Sadhana

With kind regards,  and prem

Sadhana

The Path of Transformation

From the teachings of Swami Sivananda Saraswati
and Swami Satyananda Saraswati

Yoga Publications Trust, Munger, Bihar, India

Published by Yoga Publications Trust
First edition 2011

ISBN: 978-93-81620-04-5

Publisher and distributor: Yoga Publications Trust, Ganga Darshan, Munger, Bihar, India.

Website: www.biharyoga.net
www.rikhiapeeth.net

Printed at Thomson Press (India) Limited, New Delhi, 110001

Dedication

In humility we offer this dedication to
Swami Sivananda Saraswati, who initiated
Swami Satyananda Saraswati into the secrets of yoga.

Contents

Introduction

This book about sadhana is compiled from the enlightened teachings of two great Indian sages, Swami Sivananda of Rishikesh, and his disciple, Swami Satyananda. It offers a deep understanding into sadhana and provides an invaluable link between the practitioner of sadhana and the revealed knowledge of the spiritual masters.

In these teachings, Swami Sivananda and Swami Satyananda clearly explain that the basis for all spiritual sadhana is the personal evolution of the sadhaka. They talk about sadhana as a spiritual quest, as a means of shifting one's superficial perspective of life into a higher dimension so that every moment of life can be dedicated to higher ideals. The ultimate purpose of sadhana is concerned only with practical ways of unfolding and awakening the potential already existing in every person's being and transforming life into an expression of joy. Sadhana aims at developing an integrated personality, developing better control over the mind and making it more creative. These teachings illustrate how sadhana is a practical method to completely overhaul the instinctive nature and to gain mastery over all circumstances by facing them and learning how to resolve them in a positive, uplifting and peaceful manner. The details of how this process of transformation unfolds are also discussed.

Inspiration, guidance and advice relevant to the various temperaments of aspirants interested in sadhana are an integral feature of these teachings. Furthermore, the teachings are down to earth and realistic; they are a special gift to all who practise sadhana as they encourage proper understanding and support all who take up the spiritual quest to reach higher stages of sadhana.

Each chapter reveals a wealth of insight into the important aspects of the purpose, necessity and practice of sadhana. The foundations of sadhana are considered, including faith, satsang, self-study, transcending the intellect and mental equilibrium. The fundamental requisites of heightened awareness, inner silence, strength of will and endurance, regularity and continuity of practice, and the gift of God's grace are explained in a manner that will enhance the sadhana of the experienced and provide valuable essentials for the beginner.

A sincere aspirant will definitely come across obstacles which are a natural outcome of the mind's entry into spiritual life. In the face of such obstacles even the most experienced sadhakas may falter, become disillusioned and waver in their convictions. However, the perspective of the enlightened masters gives insight into the meaning of purification and such obstacles are viewed as divine chances that help to purge foreign matter from the soul. Whatever experiences are undergone are all a part of sadhana, not detrimental to it. Sadhakas are reminded that God creates every event with a great purpose behind it.

Specific sadhanas illustrate the teachings, and a variety of sadhanas are also explained, including remembering God's name, japa, prayer, mouna, kirtan, the four yogas, keeping a spiritual diary, etc. However, the recommendation that all sadhana practices be learnt from an experienced teacher is also given to ensure that harmful side effects are avoided. Welcome words of warning and caution highlight both the major and minor pitfalls on the path of sadhana. Patience, perseverance, vigilance, sincerity and earnestness are required at every step of the way. However, special emphasis is given to the role of guru who initiates one into sadhana and then

2

gives the inspiration to remain on the path. The teachings explain how the process of sadhana takes the aspirant through the deepest layers of the mind, where all the impressions of past experiences are encountered. To maintain equilibrium at this point of sadhana, the guidance of an experienced guru is essential. However, remember that the guidance and advice of experienced masters is always available to those who seek it.

Every sadhaka has a particular karma, personality, desires, passions, idiosyncrasies and infirmities. In the scheme of evolution, everyone is standing at a particular point. It is from that point that sadhana must be begun. Aspirants are encouraged not to be in too much of a hurry. Rather progress should be slow but sure, which will allow the body, mind and emotions to adjust to new and more refined levels of functioning. After all is said and done, sadhana is a sacred act, something to be held in great reverence.

Swami Sivananda and Swami Satyananda remind practitioners of sadhana that they have a responsibility to try their utmost to maintain the spiritual meaning of sadhana. Sadhakas must aspire to eventually carry the higher spiritual values of life, cultivated in sadhana, into every situation. Sadhana is to be practised for the sake of all creation. Although the aspiration for self-perfection is necessary, it must be combined with an interest in the welfare of other beings and the environment in which one lives. There has to be regard for oneself and others.

Ultimately, the truth of what has been revealed in this book can only be verified through personal experience and, for that, one must take the plunge into sadhana and begin to pick up the threads which link the events of one's life and give it a definite structure, beauty and divine purpose.

In the words of Swami Satyananda, "First of all, understand what sadhana stands for. For seekers of truth, sadhana comes as the means to higher spiritual realization, for the experience of bliss, ananda. This state of experience is the ultimate goal of everybody. Sadhana is not meant for magic mongering or mystifying the unwary. It is for spiritual wellbeing, and comes as a blessing for suffering humanity.

Do you enjoy a happy and harmonious home life? Are you afire with enthusiasm in your day to day activities? When adverse circumstances squash and suppress you, do you rise above them with a cool head and easy assurance? If so, you are a yogi. Through sadhana, strive to put your house in order. Strive with every fibre of your being for the betterment of society and the welfare of humanity."

Sadhana

From the teachings of Swami Sivananda Saraswati

1

Light on Sadhana

Sadhana is unfolding the latent capacities of the soul. It is a lifelong process and the purpose for which the human being has come into the world. Sadhana is the process of transforming the imperfect, limited human personality into the original, unlimited splendour of perfect divinity. Sadhana is the secret of success on the spiritual path. Just as butter can be extracted from milk only after churning, similarly, if the *sadhaka*, the spiritual aspirant who practises sadhana, wants to realize God, *sadhana*, spiritual practice or discipline, must be performed regularly and constantly in earnest.

Sadhana is real wealth, the only thing of real and ever-lasting value. The practice of sadhana will strengthen the character of the aspirant and help to gain mastery over any circumstances by facing them fairly and solving them honestly. Long discipline and intense struggle have conferred upon saints and sages the power of seeing that highest reality which worldly people cannot see. Through the process of sadhana man's divine nature unfolds and is able to find positive expression in the intellectual, emotional and physical aspects of life, on individual as well as social planes. Yet, always remember that no soul can grow without aspiration, renunciation, discrimination, dispassion and meditation. Therefore, take up sadhana with determination and longing.

Sadhana is discipline of the mind, senses and physical body. Through sadhana one can have complete mastery over

7

the mind, passions, emotions, impulses, temper, tongue and so forth. The body and mind will be ever at one's beck and call. Regular spiritual practice gives calmness of mind at all times. It can help in business life as well as in daily life, and give restful sleep. Sadhana helps in the coordination and control of the subtle forces within the body. The aspirant can have increased energy, vigour, vitality, longevity and a high standard of health, and turn out efficient work within a short space of time. Success can be had in every walk of life. Sadhana will infuse the aspirant with new strength, confidence and self-reliance. Success in sadhana brings perfection, peace and everlasting happiness.

However, many hardships and privations have to be faced for the successful practice of sadhana. Spiritual growth is gauged by victory over external circumstances, troubles and difficulties. *Titiksha*, endurance, develops willpower. *Vairagya*, dispassion or indifference to enjoyments, is an essential factor in controlling the attachment to sense objects. With mental detachment from worldly objects, even a householder with a large family can do spiritual sadhana amidst worldly activities. Aspirants should bear patiently the pairs of opposites such as heat and cold, pain and pleasure. That is why in the *Bhagavad Gita*, (2:14–15), Lord Krishna tells Arjuna: "The contacts of the senses with objects which cause heat and cold, pleasure and pain have a beginning and an end; they are impermanent. Endure them bravely. He whom these do not torment, to whom pleasure and pain are the same, is fit to attain immortality."

Essence of sadhana

The essence of sadhana is to behold the supreme and rest in divinity. Real sadhana is seeing God in everything and transmuting evil into good. It will rend asunder all the fetters of ignorance, and one will abide in eternity. Through sadhana a realm is reached where there is neither light nor darkness, neither east nor west, neither gain nor loss – a realm which can never be reached by the mind or the senses. It is not an imaginary region, but the one and the only eternal abode of perennial peace and deep, abiding joy, wherein this fluctuating, restless mind can find permanent rest. Sages like Shankara, Dattatreya, Mansoor, Gargi, Chudalai, Jesus and others reached this destination after strenuous struggle and exertion. The possibility of reaching the same level is within the reach of all who are ready to struggle hard with patience, perseverance, iron determination and strong will. In perfected sadhana, the aspirant relinquishes all thoughts of objects other than God, and forgets his own existence. Practise sadhana to attain higher spiritual realization; do not neglect it. The lives of great ones are reminders that one can make one's life sublime. Always keep pictures of saints and sages at hand.

Sadhana is any spiritual practice that helps the aspirant to attain the goal of human life, to attain perfection, to realize God. Sadhana is steadying the mind and fixing it on the Lord. The ways of sadhana differ according to the temperament, tendencies and capacities of the individual aspirant, but remember that all paths lead to the same goal.

Different stages of mental development and varying degrees of spiritual evolution naturally require different practices as the basis of sadhana. The jnani sees the one self in all; the bhakta visualizes his deity in all; and the karma yogi or the raja yogi subscribes to either of the above two. Bhaktas start their sadhana with devotion, faith and self-surrender. Higher emotions play a conspicuous part in their sadhana and they express their compassion for mankind in selfless service. Jnana yogis start their sadhana by enquiring into the higher mind and divine will. Tantrics start their sadhana with shakti.

Hatha yogis start their sadhana with the body and prana, by practising asana, mudra, bandha and pranayama. Their theory is that by controlling prana, the mind can be controlled. Raja yogis start their sadhana directly with the mind. They control the vrittis; they make the mind blank. Gradually they take up the practice of dharana and dhyana in sadhana.

9

They improve the quality of the mind by practising yama and niyama.

Behind worldly names and forms, behind the fleeting sense objects, behind the perishable phenomena, there is the *satchidananda para brahman*, full of bliss, eternal peace and wisdom, illumination and enlightenment. Attain this *atman*, the supreme soul, through sadhana, through studying sacred scriptures, meditation, japa, kirtan and satsang. Practise the ashtanga yoga of Sage Patanjali; the bhakti yoga of Sage Narada; the jnana yoga of Shankaracharya, and the karma yoga of Sri Krishna. There is also the yoga sadhana of synthesis, which is most suitable for this modern age. Sadhana will free one from the trammels of the flesh, from slavery to the mind and from the shackles of transmigration.

Purpose of sadhana

Sadhana is a not a system which can be taught and learnt through lectures or correspondence courses. Sadhana is not a subject that can be understood and realized by mere scholarly learning, intellectual study or reasoning, or even by discussions and arguments. Vast study with a high degree of intelligence alone cannot help in the practical realization of Truth. It is the regular practices, such as concentration, meditation, cultivation of fundamental virtues like truthfulness, selfless love, purity, self-restraint, etc., which constitute the main items of the aspirant's effort towards spiritual evolution.

The purpose of sadhana is to release life from the limitations with which it is bound, to free one from the thraldom of matter and the fetters of prakriti, to make one realize one's absolute independent nature. By perfecting sadhana the aspirant will be freed from birth and death, and enjoy eternal bliss. This is the goal. This is the dharma of the sadhaka. One has taken birth here as a human being in order to reach this goal here and now, in this very birth. If one does not strive to reach this goal, one is wasting one's life and neglecting God's precious gift of human birth.

The practice of sadhana helps the aspirant to control the emotions and passions and gives the power to resist temptations and remove the disturbing elements from the mind. To this end sadhana should make one ever cheerful, more concentrated, joyful, balanced, peaceful, contented, blissful, dispassionate, fearless, courageous, compassionate, angerless, 'I'-less, desireless and mineless. Sadhana should give a rich inner life, introspective inner vision and equilibrium under all conditions of life. These are the signs of spiritual growth. Seeing visions, lights, hearing transcendental sounds, etc. do not have much spiritual value, although they indicate that one has attained some small degree of concentration.

Progress in steps and stages
The process of sadhana embodies an ascent into purity, into that absolute perfection which is the original state of man. It implies removal of enveloping impurities, stilling of the vagaries of the lower mind and the establishment of a state of perfect balance and harmony. It demands perfect discipline that is acquired by sincere, sustained effort. The aspirant should live under a guru for some years and lead a rigorous

11

life of sadhana with practices of austerity, discipline and meditation. Only then can he become established in his path.

Spiritual growth is gradual. Through sadhana there is progressive evolution. There should be no a feverish hurry to accomplish great yogic feats or enter into nirvikalpa samadhi or the superconscious state, in two or three months. Rather, the aspirant will have to march on the spiritual path stage by stage. There are no shortcuts on the spiritual path. Spiritual progress is slow; spiritual sadhana is laborious. Spiritual strength is gained slowly, so be patient, persevering and steady.

A person who is sincere in sadhana can evolve quickly by great self-control and consistent determined effort. He can hasten his spiritual progress in a few births, which otherwise would take thousands of years. A first-class aspirant with extremely good spiritual *samskaras* or impressions can have higher realization within the twinkling of an eye in one birth, but this is rarely seen.

Progress in sadhana moves in steps and stages. In the first, purity of mind is achieved; in the second, the power to concentrate is greatly increased; then the third stage intervenes, where profound meditation becomes possible and easy to achieve. In the fourth stage, the aspirant gains illumination; thereafter there is identification of the inner spiritual self with the all-pervading, omniscient and omnipotent divinity. Finally there is the experience of complete absorption in the infinite supreme being.

All methods of yoga sadhana have ethical training and moral perfection as their basis. The eradication of vices and the development of certain virtues forms the first step in sadhana. Disciplining one's nature and developing a steady and pure character through a set of correct habits and regular daily observances, the *yamas* and *niyamas* of raja yoga, is the next step.

On the path of spiritual sadhana a life of inactivity carries with it the danger of stagnation setting in at some stage. This is the reason why many aspirants fail to reach the ultimate spiritual state even after many years of seclusion and meditation. There must be a positive passion for putting into practice

12

the good within for the enhancement of the joy and welfare of all creatures. Only then do these virtues justify themselves, and become ripe fruits and fully blossomed flowers. If they are to gradually extend from individual sadhana to all humanity, development and progress must be dynamic. Remember that the purpose of sadhana is unfolding the divine nature by cultivating and strengthening the divine virtues inherent within. Selfless activity and loving service should therefore never be underestimated or neglected.

There are sure tests of progress in sadhana. Does spiritual life mean a matter of great delight, a delight far transcending the happiness that the world of vital pleasures affords or offers? Has one's personal awareness a sense of peace and strength in everyday life? Is there certainty that the powers of discrimination, *viveka*, and dispassion, *vairagya*, have been steadily growing? Is one's life being gradually led to experiences which reveal the operation of a higher will and intelligence? Has there come into the conscious activities of everyday life a new delightful angle of vision, a new perspective, a strong sense of self-possession, a steadily growing conviction of dependence upon the all-pervading divinity?

If the answer is yes to any one of these questions, be sure that one is progressing in sadhana. Peace, cheerfulness, contentment, dispassion, fearlessness and an unperturbed state of mind under all conditions indicate that the aspirant is advancing in sadhana. Real spiritual progress is not measured by *siddhis*, psychic powers, but by the serenity, calmness and tranquillity manifested in the waking state. Even so, as one progresses on the spiritual path by the grace of guru and God, all the intricate problems of life and death will be seen to dissolve into the ever-abiding Truth of existence.

Need for yoga sadhana

Man is a complex social animal with a multiplicity of interests, yet philosophically speaking he is the image of God, Brahman Himself. He has lost his divine glory by tasting the fruit of the 'forbidden tree'. That lost divinity can be regained by mental discipline and the practice of sadhana. Removing the vrittis and impurities of the mind is the most important sadhana. By making a constant effort to fix the mind on God, non-attachment towards sense objects can be developed. The wandering mind must be controlled by steady practice and dispassion, by sticking to one place, one preceptor and one progressive method of sadhana.

Why shouldn't the aspirant claim his divine birthright and break his worldly bondage now? It is in his power to do it now. Delay means prolonging suffering, so do vigorous sadhana to attain freedom, immortality, and eternal bliss. Make the lower nature the servant of the higher, through discipline, self-restraint and meditation. This is the beginning of freedom.

Practise sadhana to conquer the lower self or mind and attain knowledge of the higher self. Sensual objects have been enjoyed in millions of births, and for many years in this birth, but still one is not yet satisfied. How long will one run after the mirage of sensual objects and be deluded by the senses? Practise sadhana. Only by developing dispassion and renunciation, and realizing the soul, the *atman*, will eternal satisfaction, everlasting peace and immortal bliss be attained. Wake up from the slumber of ignorance.

So long as the senses are not subdued or weakened, regular sadhana will have to be practised, including self-restraint, restraint of the senses or *pratyahara*. Sit down with a composed mind. Assert one's mastery over the body and mind. Plunge deep into the chambers of the heart, and enter into the stupendous ocean of silence. Listen to the voice which is soundless. Sadhana is the only means to accomplish this.

There must be the habit of doing sadhana daily. Practise a sadhana which includes mouna, have a light diet or a diet of milk and fruits, and live in solitude with charming scenery. Live unattached in the world. Seclusion and silent meditation are necessary for spiritual growth. Sadhana should be regular and systematic: asana, pranayama, japa, meditation practice, study of the *Bhagavad Gita*, Upanishads and *Viveka Chudamani*, and selfless service.

14

Every attempt on the spiritual path, however feeble, will add to inner spiritual strength. Little acts of virtue, doing something useful for others, little acts of purity, doing japa and studying the scriptures will help a lot in sadhana. Prayer, kirtan and meditation will open the gates to the domain of inner freedom and eternal bliss. Strive ceaselessly and attain success. If one persists in sadhana vigorously and diligently, if one is regular, systematic and punctual in sadhana, success will be attained. Even to visualize the Lord in meditation just once or to utter the divine name of the Lord with pure emotion a single time surely has a tremendous, transforming influence upon the soul.

The aspirant should be contented with whatever comes by chance and apply himself to sadhana with a dispassionate mind. Spiritual life should be built on a sure foundation, on the rock of divine grace and strength of character. Practise sadhana and walk with a definite aim. Climb the hill of knowledge steadily and reach the summit of the temple of Brahman or the sweet abode of immortality.

Guru's grace and guidance

A guru is absolutely necessary for every aspirant on the spiritual path. For progress in higher spiritual sadhana, personal contact with a guru, practising under his guidance and receiving his grace is imperative. For success in sadhana, guru's grace and guidance are essential. This does not mean that the disciple should sit idle and expect a miracle from the guru to push him directly into samadhi. The guru cannot do sadhana or spiritual practice for the aspirant. He can guide the aspirant, help to clear away doubts, throw light on the path to remove obstacles that are certain to arise, but the disciple will have to carefully place each footstep on the spiritual path and on to each and every rung of the ladder.

The spiritual path is not like writing an MA thesis. A teacher's help is necessary at every moment. Young aspirants become self-sufficient and self-assertive, thinking they are in the fourth state of consciousness when they do not even know the ABC of spiritual life. As a result they do not grow; they lose faith in the efficacy of their sadhana and in the existence of God. The aspirant who lives according to the instructions of the guru can make real spiritual progress. A beginner cannot have God as his guru to begin with. The guidance of a guru who has already trodden the path is essential.

Whether one is a beginner on the spiritual path or an aspirant doing higher sadhana, a guru is a necessity. It is very difficult to find one's own way on the spiritual path, as the mind will mislead the aspirant at every turn. The guru will explain the ambiguities of the scriptures and reveal the essence of the teachings. He will find out one's defects, as due to egoism the aspirant cannot see his own errors. Satsang with a guru is like an armour to guard against temptations on the path of sadhana. The guru will be able to remove the pitfalls and lead the aspirant along the right path of sadhana. He will say, "This road leads to moksha, this one to bondage." Only an illumined soul can enlighten another soul.

2

Foundations of Sadhana

There are six means upon which the foundations of sadhana are established. They are *satsang* or association
with the wise; discrimination between the real and the unreal by enquiring 'Who am I?'; transformation of the ego by
cultivating virtues; regular and systematic practice; constant
remembrance of God; and the practice of meditation. These
are the means to unfold the inner propensities and behaviour
of all who aspire to practise sadhana. They are the means to
transmute one's nature from the instinctive level of sensual
urges to the human level of reason and discrimination, and
from the human level to the intuitive level of inner spiritual
experience and perception. They constitute the means for
realizing the higher self.

Satsang

Satsang is keeping company with evolved souls who tread the
path of Truth. It is keeping the company of saints and devotees
of God and listening to their spiritual instructions. Satsang
gives spiritual illumination, and is essential to keep the fire of
aspiration alive. Satsang elevates the mind, overhauls worldly
samskaras and vicious thoughts, and gives a new spiritual
turn of mind. It is a shield to protect the aspirant from laps-
ing into lethargy, from gliding back into the old grooves of
sensual cravings, from forgetting the goal. Satsang is spiritual
nourishment. It is the aspirant's best friend.

17

Where there is satsang, mahatmas and great saints assemble. They remind one of the highest reality and guard against the unreal glitter of worldly objects, the formidable ocean of samsara. The spirit of advanced yogis and their glorious examples inspires and sustains. Let their soul-elevating teachings and instructions be one's guide. From satsang come practical lessons on control of the mind, concentration and meditation. which are indispensable for all spiritual aspirants. Satsang inspires and sustains the aspirant, removes darkness from the mind and fills it with wisdom. It teaches not to get attached to worldly things, which pass away soon and are not real. God alone is real.

Regular attendance at satsang will compel the aspirant to lead a pure and divine life. It will remove all the clouds of the mind, and enable one to take refuge in God. Satsang will give strength when faith begins to falter. If satsang with living souls is not possible, study books by great souls. Studying the holy scriptures and the writings of saints and sages is to be in communion with the authors.

The real *satsang bhavan*, the place where satsang is held, is in one's own heart. There dwells the *Sat*, the supreme reality, that existence Absolute. It can be entered daily through the sadhana of self-analysis, introspection and self-enquiry. This will gradually lead to the ultimate goal, oneness with that infinite eternal existence. However, maya is very powerful, and even with good intentions, this foremost duty will be forgotten. Therefore, attend satsang and associate with saints and yogis who will give instructions in the practices of sadhana: yama, niyama, asana, pranayama, and how to wean the mind away from sensual objects. Satsang will inspire and give guidance on how to make the mind one-pointed by the practice of pratyahara and dharana, how to fill the mind with sattwa, and then how to meditate on the higher self, the atman dwelling in the heart.

Self-enquiry

To become established in sadhana, the aspirant must develop *viveka*, discrimination. It is acquired through *atma vichara*, enquiring into the nature of the self. This is the means to the highest form of sadhana. Through the grace of God, viveka dawns in one who has done virtuous actions in previous births as offerings to the Lord without any expectation of fruits and without egoism. Viveka is discrimination between the real and the unreal, the permanent and the non-permanent, sentient and insentient. Vichara is asking "Who am I? What is my real *swaroopa*, or essential nature? What is the atman?" Ask for that instruction by which the unheard becomes heard, the unperceived becomes perceived and the unknown becomes known. Only then will the real knowledge of sadhana be obtained.

Why read many books? The great book is within in one's heart. Open the pages of this inexhaustible volume, the source of all knowledge. Close the eyes. Withdraw the senses. Still the mind. Silence the thoughts. Make the mind waveless. Merge deep into the atman, the supreme soul. The highest truth will be revealed. Intuitional knowledge, divine wisdom, will be perceived directly. Doubts will vanish, all mental torment will disappear and all heated discussions and debates will terminate. Peace and wisdom alone will remain.

The world is mental jugglery, a mere appearance and a long dream. One is atman, spirit. Pursue sadhana to be established in this one idea. This truth must enter the bones, nerves, cells and the interior chambers of the heart. Study daily the verses of the *Ishavasya Upanishad*. Contemplate their meaning during meditation. Introspect, analyze, examine, purify and realize one's self by one's Self. For the higher Self is the supreme Lord of the little self. It is the sole refuge, source and support.

Understand the eternal law. Drive the mind back to its original home by disconnecting from the five senses, through developing *shama*, tranquillity, and *dama*, control of the senses, *pratyahara*, withdrawing the mind from the senses, *dharana*, concentration, and *dhyana*, meditation. The senses are illusory superimpositions due to ignorance; they are the five jugglers of maya. It is the highest Self or pure consciousness, one's own Self, which gives them light and power. To know the higher Self is the only duty of the sadhaka, the purpose of taking birth in a human body. In reality one is the all-pervading essence, the light of lights.

Repetition of Om, *pranava japa*, with contemplation and reverence, is one method of self-enquiry. The other is the *sakshi* or witnessing method. The aspirant separates himself from outside objects and the various vrittis inside, and becomes the sakshi, the witness, of the vrittis. This kind of sadhana can also be practised during work. Repeat constantly *Om sakshi, Om sakshi*. Do not have any particular attachment to the body. Identify with Brahman, the all-pervading reality.

See nothing but God everywhere, within and without, above and below, and all around. Change the angle of vision and the mental attitude. Give up identification with the body and mineness. This world, body and mind are unreal. In reality, one is the real supreme Self. If the mind rests in the atman, doubtless one is *sukhi, shanta* and *mukta*, happy, peaceful and free. One will have heaven on earth.

20

In stillness feel the atman. In activity manifest spiritual glory and peace. Remain unruffled amidst troubles and tribulations. Life and sadhana should become one. Peel off layer after layer, and discover the eternal, immortal atman within. "I am that all-pervading atman which is one, without parts, indivisible, the Self of all beings" – try to become established in this attitude. Only then will the restlessness of the mind vanish and eternal bliss come. This is the essence to take the aspirant to the heights of sadhana.

Constant remembrance

Remembrance of the Lord through repetition of His name is *naam smarana*. It is an unbroken sadhana of remembering the name and form of the Lord, where the mind does not think of any object of the world, where the mind is ever engrossed in the thought of the glorious Lord alone. The mind meditates on what is heard about the glories of the Lord and His virtues and names, and forgets even the body.

Remembrance also includes listening to stories of the Lord, talking of Him, teaching others about Him and meditating on His attributes. Through sadhana the subconscious depths can be modified, controlled and influenced. Subconscious life is more powerful than the ordinary life of objective consciousness. All habits originate and are embedded in the subconscious. Therefore, life should be based upon ceaseless remembrance of the divine ideal and feeling His presence constantly. Do not rack the brain with problems beyond the reach of the intellect.

There is no particular time for practising remembrance of God. He is to be remembered at all times without any break, from the time of waking in the morning until completely overpowered by sleep at night. This sadhana alone can destroy all worldly impressions and turn the mind away from sense objects. Regular repetition of the Lord's name will remove scepticism and infuse faith and devotion. It is the principal sadhana in Kali yuga, the present age, and the master key to success in life and God-realization.

21

Developing the technique of constant remembrance of one's spiritual ideal will enable the aspirant to withstand adverse forces and not react to them. There may be many breaks in the beginning, but repeated practice gradually leads to constant remembrance. The company of sincere devotees is an auxiliary to the remembrance of God. Serving evolved souls is another necessity. The mind cannot but remember divine things when it is in the company of divine people.

Japa, repeating a mantra or the names of the Lord, is an important sadhana. A mantra is divinity; it has an indescribable power. Practising japa alone can give eternal peace. Japa ultimately results in communion with the Lord. Repeat the name of one's *ishta devata* or chosen deity whenever there is leisure time. Have regular times for japa, morning and evening. Pray to God at bedtime also. Always keep a japa mala in the pocket, around the neck or under the pillow at night. Mantra generates special vibrations in the body, mind and atmosphere, which are highly beneficial for sadhana.

Repetition of the Lord's name enables the devotee to feel the divine presence, the divine consciousness within and around. Singing His name and hearing its sound in kirtan raises the unconscious to sublime spiritual heights. In Kali yuga, sankirtan is an ideal sadhana to bring one the vision of God. Sing the mahamantra: *Hare Rama Hare Rama, Rama Rama Hare Hare; Hare Krishna Hare Krishna, Krishna Krishna Hare Hare*. How powerful is God's name!

All mantras are powerful. The Durga mantra will invoke the Mother's grace very speedily. Meditate day and night on that omnipresent power, Mother – the cause and the support of everything. Maya will vanish; true light will dawn. Constantly repeat inspiring verses in praise of God's glory, or some mantras, or the name of God. Have them as the divine background thought. Pray to the Lord from the core of the heart: "I am Yours. All is Yours. Thy will be done. I am an instrument in Your hands. Grant me faith and devotion." Remember the verse in the *Gita* (18:66): "Abandoning all duties, take refuge in Me (the Lord) alone, and I will liberate you from all sins; grieve not."

22

Whenever inspiration is required, read good spiritual books or write the ishta mantra or guru mantra in a notebook with a one-pointed mind. Have constant naam smarana. Even when working, mentally repeat *Sri Ram, Sri Ram*. Keep a pocket *Gita* and read it whenever there is time, a notebook for *likhit japa*, mantra writing, or a mala on which to chant one's mantra. Think of God on waking and just before going to sleep. How can one ever feel lonely when the only true friend, God, resides in one's heart? His company, through prayer, japa, kirtan and meditation is elevating, and gives unending peace, bliss and power. One will delight in the company of the sweet Lord.

Transform the little ego

Spirituality means growing into the form of the divine ideal, which comes about only through prolonged sadhana. The sadhana for the spiritual aspirant is to transform the human nature into a divine nature. Good intentions must be backed up by good actions. The secret of sadhana is renunciation of egoism, mineness and desires. Real renunciation is not abandoning family, children, property, house, relations and friends. It is mineness, *mamata*, not objects, which binds one to the perpetual cycle of birth and death. All troubles and miseries are due to egoism. Egoism limits the aspirant. The cause of misery does not come from without.

From the very beginning of spiritual life it must be understood clearly that all hopes of progress rest upon a sincere and consistent effort to gradually cultivate virtues such as courage, love, forgiveness, humility, contentment, frankness, honesty, mercy and universal love. Develop the virtue that is lacking the most. Take up one virtue a month and meditate on it regularly and in time it will manifest in the character. This helps to root out defects of pride, egoism, anger, greed and jealousy. Sadhana cannot be practised in earnest by clinging to the old little self, old habits and old self-assertive lower nature. The lower nature must be changed, as it stands in the way of the descent of divine light and becomes a serious obstacle on the path of sadhana.

If this little ego or human personality persists in retaining its petty, limited human consciousness or if the aspirant refuses even to admit the need for any change, no real spiritual advancement can be made. To grow in yoga always feel that one is just a beginner. Always think, "What I know is very little. It is only a handful of knowledge." Only then will there be intense aspiration or yearning for further knowledge.

The mind cannot exist without desire, attachment and egoism. It will cling to some form or other, entertain some desire or other. Entertaining sattwic desires and having a strong desire to attain salvation can destroy worldly desires. Instead of allowing the mind to become attached to worldly forms, try to fix it on the form of Lord Krishna or Lord Rama. Develop sattwic egoism by asserting "I am the servant of the Lord."

Power, name, fame and wealth stiffen the ego, and strengthen the worldly personality. Renounce them to attain success in sadhana. Desire for *siddhis*, psychic powers, will act like puffs of air which may blow out the lamp of spirituality that is being carefully tended. Carelessness or selfish desires will diminish the little spiritual light that the sadhaka has kindled after so much struggle and will hurl him down into the deep abyss of ignorance. Temptations are simply waiting to overwhelm the unwary student. Various psychic siddhis and other powers come to the yogi who has controlled his senses, prana and mind, but all these are hindrances, stumbling blocks, to self-realization.

Pure divine life, a life of yoga sadhana, cannot coexist with a mundane life of passion and ignorance. One may aspire for the highest truth, be endowed with devotion and possess a will to overcome obstacles and hostile forces, but if the little ego asserts or persists, rapid progress on the spiritual path is not possible. Divine life cannot conform to one's own little standards. Through sadhana one must rise above the petty human level to a higher level of divine consciousness. Do not brood over past mistakes.

Strive to acquire the primary virtues of kindness, generosity, patience, forbearance, serenity, compassion, etc. to attain

24

success in sadhana. Be ready to serve others with humility and put up with provocation and abuse without retaliation. Rise above reproach and honour, and identify with the supreme Self. Continue sadhana with an undaunted heart.

Live only to be a blessing to others, by building up good habits, looking within and trying to correct one's defects. This is real sadhana. Courtesy and politeness must become part of one's very essence. Only then will the hardened heart become softened and will good sentiments and spiritual energy arise. Where there is kindness, humility and purity, spirituality springs up, saintliness shines, divinity descends and perfection manifests. These divine qualities are a consummation of all that is best in the human nature and help to transcend the little ego. Be soft, simple, pure and childlike. Walk and talk with the Lord. Cope with anything that comes. Pray and meditate. Only then is one open to the currents of the spiritual flood of transcendental divinity.

Ahimsa, non-violence, *satya*, truthfulness, and *brahmacharya*, continence and purity, are most important virtues for purifying the ego. If an aspirant is established in one of these virtues, the others will also cling to him. Watch the vrittis. Introspect. In the beginning, practise at least physical purity and later mental purity will come by itself. An unpleasant truth is better left unsaid. Not hurting and wounding the feelings of others is equally as important as speaking the truth. Satya and ahimsa must go together. Violence, in any form, is not permissible under any circumstances, at any time, or place, or for any purpose whatsoever. Forgive those who slander or speak ill of one's self or others and greet them courteously.

If thoughts of jealousy, greed, passion or pride enter the mind, be indifferent. Do not use willpower to drive them out, as loss of energy and fatigue will result. The greater the effort made, the more the negative thoughts will return with redoubled force. They will pass away soon if they are not fed with feelings and ideas. Substitute good counter-thoughts – this is *pratipaksha bhavana*. Or think of the picture of God or guru and one's mantra again and again. Or pray. Study oneself. Be good. Do good. Be gentle. Be generous. Develop the inner eye of wisdom through regular sadhana. Attain spiritual realization through satsang, swadhyaya, japa, kirtan and meditation.

Be regular, systematic and punctual

The fruit of sadhana cannot come immediately. Spiritual evolution is gradual. Regularity in sadhana is of paramount importance; it is the means to attain the ideal spiritual goal. A person who is irregular and does actions in fits and starts cannot reap the fruits of his efforts. If one persists in sadhana diligently, if one is regular, systematic and punctual in sadhana, success will be attained.

In the *Yoga Sutras* (1:14), Sage Patanjali says that sadhana practice must be steady and continuous; it must stretch over a considerable period, and be undertaken with perfect faith in its regenerating and uplifting powers. Do not slacken at any stage of sadhana. If there is carelessness and irregularity in sadhana, if dispassion wanes, if sadhana is given up for some days due to laziness, adverse forces will quickly take one away from the true path. The good results which have been achieved may be blown away and it will be very difficult to rise up again to the original heights. Therefore, be very regular in spiritual practice, whether it is japa, asana, pranayama or meditation, and do it systematically every day. It will give new strength and an inner life of joy and bliss, despite stormy conditions and adverse circumstances.

Sadhana requires patience. Just as a gardener who waters the trees daily gets the fruits only when the time comes, so too the aspirant will enjoy the fruits of sadhana only when the time comes. The *Bhagavad Gita* (6:25) says: "Little by little gain tranquillity, by steady and regular practice." Therefore, be persistent and methodical in sadhana. Let the sadhana be constant and unbroken. Not only regularity but continuity is necessary to attain higher spiritual awareness quickly. A spiritual stream once set going does not dry up unless the channel is blocked, unless there is stagnation.

26

There must be an ideal and aim in life. It can be realized now through determination, or after ten years by walking with faltering steps. Words like 'cannot', 'difficult', 'impossible' and 'weak' have no place in the life of a serious sadhaka. Sadhana must be regular, continuous, unbroken and earnest. Remember that determination is advocated in respect of truly high and noble principles and not of self-conceited notions. Stick to spiritual yogic *yamas* or self-restraints and *niyamas* or personal disciplines, but avoid becoming obstinate. Do not be deceived. Watch the mind! Sadhana is a series of awakenings. Gradually one will grow spiritually. One will attain eternal bliss.

Meditation

Meditation helps to overcome worldly thoughts, increases harmony and steadiness, gives good health, destroys rebirths, and gives peace and bliss. The ultimate truth or Brahman can be experienced by everyone through regular meditation practice with a pure heart. Regular meditation opens the avenues of intuitional knowledge, makes the mind calm and steady, awakens an ecstatic feeling and brings the aspirant in contact with the source or the supreme Purusha. Meditation acts like dynamite and blows up all the thoughts and memories in the subconscious mind.

During meditation, aim to have one continuous flow of thought of God alone. Fix the mind on the form of Lord Hari or any deity according to one's liking. Again and again try to call up this mental image. All other thoughts will die by themselves. However, there is no use jumping to meditation without having done the preliminary practices and purifying the heart. Those people who have not practised any yogic discipline to manage the senses and impurities of the mind will find it difficult to practise meditation as well as concentration. Therefore, alongside meditation practices one needs to be fully engaged in the daily practice of karma yoga, selfless service.

Sleep is a great obstacle in meditation. The aspirant will have to be careful and vigilant. A light diet at night will help in meditation. Restlessness, scepticism, sleep, laziness, mind-wandering, ill-will, hatred, anger, desire for sexual enjoyment are all definite hindrances to meditation. If concentration and meditation are practised amidst unfavourable environments, one will grow strong, develop willpower quickly and become a dynamic personality.

When outside sounds are not heard, when ideas of the body and surroundings disappear, when inner unruffled peace manifests, one is said to enter the first degree of deep meditation. Ignore the experiences that may arise and march forward to the goal which is the source of all phenomena, which transcends all experiences.

Repeat one's mantra and constantly gaze at the chosen deity or any symbol that fills one with reverence and devotion. As one progresses in sadhana the form will gradually become clear in the mind. Repeating some prayers, slokas and stotras before starting japa or meditation will elevate the mind quickly. The practice of meditation will eventually lead a sadhaka to the summit of sadhana, superconsciousness. All worldly miseries will be destroyed totally, and one will rest in the highest state of bliss.

3

Qualifications for Success
in Sadhana

Solid spiritual practice is necessary to thoroughly overhaul the worldly nature. Becoming absolutely fearless is the sign of life in the atman, the spirit. Wanting a spiritual pill or a talisman to attain self-realization, or wanting spiritual powers to drop from heaven are all foolish ideas. The aspirant will have to do all the practices of sadhana himself, without depending on others.

Sadhana requires patience, great perseverance like that of the bird which ventured to empty the ocean with its beak, leech-like tenacity and gigantic and adamantine will. Anything can be achieved through right endeavour. People with insight into the true nature of the world have discerned the truth about the world by lifting themselves up and freeing themselves from endless cravings for worldly objects by their own self-efforts and exertion. Do not sit idle, craving God's help, but be up and doing, for God helps only those who help themselves.

The aspirant must work out his own salvation in right earnest. The guru can only guide one in the right direction. The aspirant will have to climb each step of the evolutionary ladder. Never complain about lack of opportunity. Where there is a will, there is a way. If one is really sincere in one's efforts, opportunities will be created by themselves. The Lord's grace comes to those who exert in right earnest.

It is very difficult to find an aspirant who cares for nothing but final liberation, and who treats the whole world and its contents as mere dry straw, and who meditates incessantly upon how to attain salvation from embodied existence. To realize the highest truth, one must live it. The desire to know the truth springs only in the person whose mind is pure, who is free from desires and who, freed from deeds in this birth and in previous ones, becomes disgusted with external, ephemeral, perishable objects. One must grow into the very form of truth. Not a partial but a perfect and comprehensive adherence to truth is the first element in forming the foundation of the sadhaka's life.

Control over passion constitutes the essence of truth and spiritual sadhana. To restrain the senses, to speak the truth, to love all as one's own self is the essence of sadhana. To be dispassionate and pure in thought, word and deed, to be contented and cheerful, to be undeluded, ever vigilant and to remember God ceaselessly is the essence of sadhana. An aspirant must set foot and proceed on the path of sadhana with firm faith, practical application, perseverance, careful attention to even small details and fortitude in trials. The divine within is stronger than anything outside. Therefore, do not be afraid of anything. Unflinching faith puts the aspirant in touch with the infinite. Tap the source by looking within.

Faith

Spiritual progress depends on faith in God, scriptures and guru. It is more difficult to place faith in the spiritual realm, with its unseen laws and effects, than in mathematics or science. But initial faith is necessary. Even doing sincere sadhana for one full year will give some experience, some concrete evidence to convince one of the presence of an unseen power. The more the sadhana, the greater the experience. With every increase in faith, the more sadhana is done. Sadhana is prescribed to induce faith.

Most people have not yet learnt to take up sadhana because they do not really believe it is necessary. Hundreds of spiritual books are read, discourses attended and gatherings convened specifically on the theme of sadhana. After years of intense study of spiritual books, contact with saints, after hearing these things again and again, yet people do not actually do anything, because they have no deep and abiding faith in the words of saints, in the scriptures, in the words of those who have trodden the path and attained bliss. Faith in external objects is more real. It is this basic lack of faith that is at the root of the failure to do sadhana

Faith is an essential prerequisite for spiritual sadhana. However much one argues, one cannot understand the nature of God. Faith leads to peace and harmony. Faith reflects God; intellect veils Him. God is the hand that holds the torch of intellect; it is useless trying to apply intellect to the truth of His existence. Faith in the existence of God and faith in the words of saints and sages is required. This will lead to inner peace and stillness in sadhana, and in that peace and stillness one will discover God.

Abhyasa and perseverance

After gaining full faith in the words of the seers and knowing the necessity of sadhana comes *abhyasa*, practice with perseverance. Once sadhana is commenced, it should not be given up easily, but persevered with; otherwise nothing can be achieved. Sadhana should be continued until perfection is attained, until one is able to turn the mind inward, change its outgoing tendencies, take it back to its source, and absorb it in the atman. This is known as abhyasa.

Abhyasa means to practise regularly, for a long time without any break and with perfect devotion and reverence. This allows the sadhana to become fixed and steady so that something concrete can be attained from one's efforts and experiences. Constant steady application is indispensable for perfect control of the mind and attainment of asamprajnata samadhi, which alone can burn up all the seeds of samskaras. The sadhaka must not give up until the ultimate fruit is obtained.

While persevering, courage is needed not to be easily shaken by obstacles, to brave the storms and proceed in spite

31

of the difficulties and adverse conditions trying to push one off the path of sadhana. In spiritual sadhana, the aspirant does not have to contend merely with positive forces. There are active forces that oppose him, that actually assail him and pull him down. Herein comes the necessity of fortitude, with which the aspirant refuses to be discouraged and proceeds with the sadhana, relying on the inner self.

Sometimes the mind rebels against monotony, becomes disgusted with one kind of sadhana and wants another kind of practice. The aspirant should know how to coax the mind on such occasions and to extract the best from it. Stopping sadhana is a grave blunder. Spiritual practices should never be given up under any circumstances. If sadhana is stopped prematurely, the mind will become the devil's workshop. Do not expect anything, but be sincere and regular. Do not deviate from the chosen path. One's efforts will be surely crowned with roaring success. It takes a long time to purify the mind and achieve one-pointedness in sadhana, so be cool and patient.

The mind has the capacity to make a hell out of heaven and a heaven out of hell. So never give way to negative or depressive thoughts, but calmly go on with the spiritual practices. Be regular and proceed onward, without missing a day. Ultimately, the cumulative force of all the continuous, earnest sadhana done with perseverance and patience over a long period of time will have its inevitable grand consummation at the supreme moment, when it bears fruit in the form of blissful God-realization. May God grant the strength to master the mind and enjoy eternal peace.

Attention to details

Ultimately, the ideal for which one has been born upon earth will be attained. While going through this process the necessity of giving minute attention to all the small details upon the path will have to be kept in mind, because in every process the fine details need to be attended to carefully. If small details are left out, thinking that they are superfluous, one will find that ultimately valuable time and effort have been lost. This delays progress, as the conglomeration of small details in sadhana adds up to the achievement of high ideals.

Silent witness, vigilant guide
In the practice of sadhana most of the forces seekers have to contend with are mental. Therefore, while maintaining regular practices like remembering the name of God and developing virtues, or when engaged in any action, the aspirant must at the same time adopt the attitude of the silent witness. Train a portion of the mind to act as a sort of ever vigilant guide. Repeat the formula, "I am the silent witness."

As soon as any adverse feelings or emotions arise, or any thoughts detrimental to sadhana arise in the mind, stand as a silent witness. This silent witness will immediately separate one from them. Do not identify with these feelings and emotions. Identifying with them is the cause of bondage and misery. This can come only though diligent cultivation and practice.

Maintain a ceaseless search and vigorous enquiry inwardly. Watch the mind; note what the mind is doing at least once in an hour. This is the best method to find out the defects and weaknesses in the mind. Then use suitable methods to remove them. Pray to the Lord to illuminate one's intellect with the light of knowledge. Watch the mind. Watch and pray. Only through introspection, analysis, discrimination, vigilance and prayer can the subtle jugglery of this wonderful thing called 'mind' be understood and its deceptions and tricks transcended.

To know exactly where one stands on the path of sadhana is very difficult. The tricks of the mind are most subtle. Only constant reflection will keep one alert and safe. Probe into the mind. Do not be lenient with the mind. The mind will try to compromise. Relentlessly hunt out its hidden motives. Subject oneself to keen self-analysis every day without fail. Become an intelligent, serious and earnest sadhaka with introspective inner vision and an unruffled state of mind under all conditions of life.

Spiritualize all activities

Feel that one is an instrument in the Lord's hands and that all the senses belong to Him. Repeat the formula: "I am Yours; all is Yours; Your Will be done." If this formula is forgotten and the ego asserts itself, introspect again and again and find out one's weakness. Try to become established in the feeling, "I am an instrument in the hands of the Lord." One will feel the spirit of *sharanagati*, self-surrender. The Lord is in one and one is in the Lord.

In this way, all activities should be spiritualized. Feel that the whole world is a manifestation of the Lord and one is serving the Lord in all names and forms. Do not identify with actions, and at the end of every day offer all actions and their fruits to God. Receive everybody in this world with love, respect, kindness and cheerfulness. Who knows in what form the Lord may appear.

Feel that the whole world is one's body, one's own home. Melt or destroy all barriers that separate one person from another. The idea of superiority is ignorance or delusion. Feel that this body is a moving temple of God. Whether at home, the office, railway station or market, feel that one is in the temple. Consecrate every act as an offering to the Lord. Transmute every work into sadhana by offering its fruits to God. Feel that all beings are images of God. Feel that one power or God works through all hands, sees through all eyes, hears through all ears. One will become a changed being, and enjoy the highest peace and bliss. By perfecting this sadhana, the heart will be purified and ready to receive the divine light and grace.

Selflessness

Selfishness is a negative attribute of the lower mind and arises in a mind filled with passion. It is the first-born child of lack of discrimination. Selfishness retards spiritual progress, contracts the heart and intensifies the idea of being separate from others. Selfishness goes hand in hand with egoism, vanity, miserliness, dishonesty and pride. Sadhana is practised in vain if one is selfish and has a miserly heart, if one has no mercy and sympathy, if one does not lead a life of virtue, austerity and meditation and if one does not help and serve charitable institutions and spiritual guides with courtesy and devotion. Develop the heart by giving.

Meditation is not possible without eradicating the selfish nature. If selfishness can be destroyed, half of one's spiritual sadhana is over. Selfishness can be eradicated by watching and analyzing the mind. Study the personality and its defects and try to remove them by suitable methods. Cultivate the opposite virtuous qualities, such as magnanimity, integrity, generosity, mercy and universal love, all of which will go a long way in eradicating selfishness, the foe of peace. Positive over-powers negative. This is an infallible dictum in sadhana.

Scrutinize the motives when interacting with others. If the aspirant wishes to become one with the universal consciousness, the heart must expand. Selfishness, jealousy, hatred and greed are barriers that separate one from the rest of the world. Sage Patanjali advocates the practice of friendship between equals, compassion towards inferiors, complacency towards superiors and indifference towards ignorant or wicked people. This practice will generate peace of mind or composure and eradicate hatred, jealousy, etc. A new life will dawn within when these virtues are practised. What is needed is persever-ance, the keynote of sadhana.

Become a karma yogi and work for the wellbeing of the world. One who lives for others truly lives. A selfish person is a dead person though he is alive. Practise pure unselfish love in daily life. Practise selfless service in some form or other: serve the sick, console the distressed. Embrace all liv-ing beings. Do not care for personal gain or remuneration. A person of good deeds and good, pleasant, sweet speech has no enemy. If one really wants spiritual growth and salvation, do good to those who attempt to poison or hurt one. Live the gospel of love. One will merge in the universal consciousness. Universal service must be done to attain that state of being one with the universal consciousness.

Worship God in the poor and the sick. Have no attachment to any place, person or thing. Make this one's sadhana. Keep up this attitude amidst the changes of the world without consideration for success or failure, gain or loss, pleasure and pain. If the mind is always rooted in the higher self amidst all activities, then one will become truly selfless, a true karma yogi.

Strong mind and body
The vessel must be strong enough to hold the divine light; otherwise it will break at any moment. That vessel is one's own mind. Prepare the mind first to receive the divine light. Get rid of mental weakness, superstitions, wrong imaginings, false fears and wrong samskaras. The vessel can become strong only if it is purified through constant, untiring selfless service, japa, kirtan, satsang, study of scriptures, meditation and pranayama.

The physical body is the holy shrine of God. It is the temple of the Lord. The body is an instrument for attaining higher spiritual awareness. Take care of the body but have no attachment to it. Keep it strong and healthy. Only then will one meet Him. Sadhana cannot be practised with a weak body. Rely on the inner self, the divinity within. All the potential for transmuting oneself into a sage is within. A little application and vigilant sadhana will ignite the spiritual dynamo within.

Uphold the ideal with firm resolve
On the path of sadhana, aspirants have to insulate themselves with aspiration and trust in God. One's spiritual ideal should become the main interest of life. It should be so firmly fixed in the mind that no matter what the adverse circumstances are, one remains unshaken and is able to continue to the end of the entire process of sadhana. The mind is so cunning that every time it is turned or directed in a particular direction, the old samskaras or vrittis become troublesome. If the aspirations are always climbing upwards towards the ideal for liberation, these forces will not be distractions.

Sadhana should not be merely a routine. Keep the divine flame burning steadily. Feed it regularly. Throw the whole heart and soul into spiritual practices. There must be earnestness to see God face to face. Develop a burning desire for the attainment of higher consciousness and burning dispassion for worldly enjoyments. Entertain noble desires and do virtuous actions. Develop an intense longing for liberation. In order to achieve this end, study the scriptures regularly and systematically. Constant satsang with the wise and study of the scriptures under a guru will slowly wipe out the old worldly samskaras. Practise right conduct, right thinking, right speaking and right acting. By and by, all the old desires, sensual cravings and negative inclinations will vanish.

If the aspirant is sincere and strong in the resolve to reach the highest goal of yoga sadhana, if there is firm determination to attain the aim of spiritual life, he will rise up again and march forward even when there are temporary falls. Sincerity in sadhana is the means to success. Nothing can stand in the way.

Realize that one is neither body nor mind, that one was never born nor will one ever die, that one is invincible and that nothing in this world can hurt one. All knowledge is within the chambers of the heart. Abandon all worldly ambitions and mundane desires. Feel the divine within. Be fully open to the divine influence. A firm resolve is the key to unlock the doors of knowledge. The path is easy for one who is dexterous, who is firm in his resolve and who has that undying aspiration to attain the highest peak of truth.

Total surrender
Desire and egoism resist surrender at every step. When there is true surrender of the whole being without the least demand, then divine grace or divine power comes flooding down into the being of the sadhaka and does the sadhana. The divine power takes complete possession of the mind, will, life and body. Then the sadhana goes on with tremendous speed. Do not keep any desire for secret gratification. The mind, chitta,

intellect and ego should all agree to surrender wholly. One will be supremely blessed. In fact, sadhana can be practised only by those who are very earnest about it and who are ready to transform their little ego and its demands. There are no half-measures on the spiritual path.

A seeker after truth or liberation must have absolute faith in his teacher and in the Upanishads. Be prepared to give full consent with the whole being to change the lower nature into a divine nature. Make total, unreserved self-surrender to the Lord or guru with heart, mind and soul. If the aspirant is not willing to receive spiritual instructions and ready to obey the orders of the guru, he remains stuck in the lower nature and cannot progress in sadhana. He must have the true spirit and attitude, and make persistent endeavours. Only then will real change come. Spiritual sadhana is not mere idle talk, not mere sensation. It is actual living in the atman, a transcendental experience of unalloyed bliss.

Avoid extremes
Man's normal nature is sensuous. The mind wants comforts and hates austerity. The undiscriminating aspirant conveniently ignores the qualifying adjective describing 'extremes' in the advice and views all austerity with disfavour. The result is he degenerates into luxury, loses even minimum determination and becomes a slave to a hundred wants. The warning is against foolish extremes, but to a sadhaka in the early stages of sadhana a certain degree of austerity is essential for development. In the *Bhagavad Gita* Lord Krishna condemned extreme, tamasic austerity, yet recommended sattwic austerity of body, mind and speech. Reflect carefully. Try to understand what is essential and what is not, and then take care only of the essentials.

The nature of man is to loath following any set lines of spiritual discipline or conduct. The sadhaka must think about the real meaning of a spiritual instruction and then determine why it has been given. Moreover, essentials and non-essentials vary according to the stage of development of the spiritual aspirant. What may be unnecessary for an aspirant at a later stage may be essential now.

Prepare gradually

Give up reading newspapers and literature which revive impression of worldly ways, agitate the mind, make one emotional and sentimental, augment the restlessness of the mind and make one forget the goal of sadhana, God. If the time spent in gossiping, daydreaming, wandering aimlessly, playing silly games, etc. is reduced, there will be ample time to do sadhana. Sadhana cannot be practised attending high society parties every day, breathing contaminated air and imbibing the noise of busy city streets, eating unnatural, heavy foods, attending cinemas, theatres and ballrooms and wasting the vital energy. Lord Krishna says, "Let the yogi constantly be engaged in yoga, remaining alone in a secret and pure place."

Willpower

Transforming the lower nature is not easy, as the force of habit is ever strong and ingrained. Great strength of will and determination are required for the achievement of higher spiritual success. The aspirant often feels helpless against the force of old habits. Sattwa and willpower will have to be developed to a considerable degree by regular japa, kirtan, meditation, untiring selfless service and satsang. When a person speaks ill of one's self or others, excuse him. Pray for him, do good to him, love him, bear insult and injury. This will develop willpower. Introspect and find out one's own defects and weaknesses. Live under the guidance of the guru, who will see the defects and point out suitable ways to eradicate them when necessary.

Stability and strong willpower will come after facing the opposing movements in life. Do not become dissatisfied with negative experiences while practising sadhana. Concentration will be gained little by little. There is no easy path to liberation except through small improvements and corrections. Do not go astray by believing the lower mind. Regular sadhana enables one to face and overcome the obstacles which may come from one's mind.

Equanimity

The foundations of sadhana can be well and truly laid only if the aspirant possesses serenity of mind to the maximum degree. An aspirant with a restless mind cannot progress in sadhana, as only a silent mind can receive and hold the divine light. Spiritual experiences will be permanent if one possesses a quiet mind; otherwise they will come and go. Unless all vain, habitual thoughts, feelings, cares, anxieties, confused ideas and imaginary fears are cast away, the mind cannot be peaceful. Set the mind free from cravings, worries, delusion, pride, lust, attachment, likes and dislikes and enter into the domain of supreme peace.

Aspirants think that they have advanced very much in meditation by sitting in a closed room for a long time. However, they are upset by trifling things. They expect respect, nice treatment, fine seats to sit on and are irritated and annoyed by petty things. They are slaves of a superiority complex, and cannot adapt to others. Hence they wander from place to place without peace of mind. Do not care for name and respect, but treat them as dust and poison because they are false and worthless. Thinking one is nothing in the world can remove pride and egoism. Always do menial service and serve others. Speak well of others and do not expose their faults. Only then will peace be attained.

Be still, quiet and tranquil under all circumstances. Only a calm mind can grasp the truth. Maintain balance and harmony between hand, heart and head, actions, feelings and thoughts. This *samatvam*, equilibrium or equanimity, is the greatest virtue for success in sadhana. Silent meditation in the morning, renouncing desires, a sattwic diet, disciplining the senses, observing silence daily for one hour – these practices will pave a long way in attaining a settled peace of mind.

Serenity is like a rock. Waves of irritation may dash on it but cannot affect it. Meditate daily on the ever-tranquil atman or the eternal which is unchanging, and attain serenity gradually. The divine light will descend only on a calm mind. One may fail many times to keep up the harmony. Stand up and struggle again and again, and success is bound to come eventually. Perseverance, tenacity, courage and determination are needed to achieve success in any sadhana.

In conclusion

For the practice of sadhana a sadhaka should have absolute regard for every creature that breathes, respect for truth, continence, austerity, absence of greed, anger and hypocrisy, and a life of contentment. Moral excellence is not the final goal of life, but only the means to that end. Only when one has purified the heart, silenced the mind, stilled the thoughts and surging emotions, withdrawn the outgoing senses and thinned out the *vasanas* or subtle desires, can one behold the glorious atman during deep meditation. Become a good person first. Self-restraint and a pure character are the prime essentials for progress in sadhana or spiritual life. Always smile and be cheerful. Think of God and meditate upon Him with true devotion and feeling.

4

Aspects of Sadhana

Brahmamuhurta, the morning period from four to six am, is very favourable for sadhana. The mind is quite refreshed, calm and serene after a good sleep. There is a preponderance of *sattwa* or purity in the mind at this time. Sattwa also predominates in the atmosphere during this period. The mind is like a blank sheet of paper and comparatively free from worldly samskaras or impressions. The currents of *raga* and *dwesha*, like and dislike, have not yet deeply entered the mind.

At this time the mind can be moulded very easily in any way one likes, and the mind can be easily charged with divine thoughts. Further, all the yogis, paramahamsas, sannyasins, aspirants and the rishis of the Himalayas start their meditation at this period and send their vibrations throughout the world. These spiritual currents will immensely benefit the aspirant. Meditation will come by itself, without any effort. It is a spiritual loss to sleep at this time and not utilize the period in divine contemplation.

Do not waste much time bathing, as brahmamuhurta passes quickly. Utilize this precious time in japa and meditation. Quickly answer the call of nature, clean the teeth and dash cold water on the face and on top of the head. This will cool the brain and the eyes. Sit in siddhasana, padmasana or sukhasana. In winter a cold bath is not necessary if unfavourable conditions prevail. A mental bath will suffice. Imagine and feel, "I am taking a bath now in the sacred rivers." Remember the pure atman. Repeat the formula, "I am the ever pure soul." This is the most powerful wisdom bath in jnana Ganga. It is highly purifying and washes away all sins.

If not in the habit of getting up early, use an alarm clock. Once the habit is established, there will be no difficulty. The subconscious mind will become a willing and obedient servant to wake one up at the particular time. It is important to do japa and meditation as soon as possible after getting out of bed. After finishing japa and meditation, asana and pranayama can be practised and the *Bhagavad Gita* and other spiritual books studied. Repeat divine *stotras* or hymns or guru stotras, or chant Om twelve times, or do kirtan for five minutes before starting japa and meditation. This will quickly elevate the mind during brahmamuhurta.

During brahmamuhurta and dusk, sushumna nadi flows readily. The mind will quieten without much effort when sushumna nadi flows. That is the reason why the rishis, yogis and scriptures speak very highly of these two periods of time. When the breath flows through both nostrils, know that sushumna is working. Whenever sushumna functions, sit for meditation and enjoy the inner peace of the atma or soul.

Diet for sadhana

Food plays a prominent role in yoga sadhana. One must be able to live on simple, easily digestible, nourishing food alone. For spiritual practices pure, sattwic food is absolutely necessary. Purity of food leads to purity of mind. Sattwic food helps in meditation. As food plays a very important role in exciting the senses and passions, aspirants should be careful to select a sattwic diet in the beginning of the sadhana period. Later, drastic dietetic restrictions can be removed. Avoid pungent foods, garlic, onion, meat, fish, alcohol, etc. Wheat, rice, barley, sugar, butter, milk, ghee, dal, vegetables and fruit are sattwic ingredients.

A nutritious mixture of boiled white rice and ghee is very conducive to sadhana practices. White rice boiled with ghee, sugar and milk is called kheer, and is also a wholesome combination suitable for sadhakas. Milk is a perfect food by itself, containing the various nutritive constituents, fats, proteins, carbohydrates, etc. in well-balanced proportions. It is an ideal food for sadhakas during extended pranayama practice. Milk should be scalded or pasteurized but not boiled. Scalding means removing the milk immediately from the fire as soon as boiling point is reached, as too much boiling destroys the vitamins and renders milk quite useless as a dietary article.

A fruit diet exercises a benign, soothing influence on the constitution and is a very desirable natural diet for practitioners. Bananas, grapes, sweet oranges, apples, pomegranates are wholesome fruits. Bananas are very nutritious. Lemons possess anti-scorbutic properties and act as restoratives for the blood. Fruit juice contains vitamin C.

Fasting checks passion, calms the emotions, controls the senses and helps in brahmacharya. It has a tremendous purifying influence on the heart. As most people are afraid of fasting too much, a regular fast on Ekadashi days or living on milk and fruit only can be undertaken. Ekadashi is the eleventh day of the lunar fortnight, a time when dietary restraints are said to be beneficial. While fasting helps in self-control, keep in mind that too much fasting weakens the body and mind and retards spiritual sadhana. Young, robust aspirants can fast up to three times per month if passion troubles them too much.

Observe moderation in diet, *mitahara*. Heavy food leads to a state of tamas and induces sleep. Moderate eating can tide over a host of ailments. Do not overload the stomach. Overeating is not conducive to yoga sadhana. Through sattwic diet one becomes a yogi. Give up those foods which the mind likes best for a fortnight in a year. Eat simple food at regular times only, in moderate quantities. At fixed regular meal times, half fill the stomach with simple, wholesome sattwic food. Quarter fill the stomach with pure water. Allow the remaining quarter to be free for expansion of gas. This is mitahara, the ideal eating pattern for all sadhakas who want to preserve their health. It is quite hygienic and is in harmony with the dietetic principles of modern medical science. In the *Bhagavad Gita* (6:16), Lord Krishna advises, "Verily, yoga is not for one who eats too much, nor one who abstains in excess . . . "

Swadhyaya

To complete the process of sadhana takes a long time, and even to become established in the preparatory steps takes a significant period. Even then, when one feels that the highest truth is within one's grasp, one must be vigilant. If the aspirant relaxes vigilance for a moment and falls into a spiritual or ethical slumber, the lower mind will assert itself. Vigilance needs to be maintained until one actually lives the highest

truth at every moment. It is not enough if the light of truth merely illumines a dark corner of one's sadhana. One of the most powerful methods of keeping the mind fully alive to the purpose of sadhana is swadhyaya.

One aspect of swadhyaya practice is daily study of the scriptures and the lives of saints, for half an hour. When reading the lives of saints and spiritual books, a host of powerful and positive ideas are fed into the mind and the mental powers are sharpened. They inspire and give one courage to conquer the lower tendencies in everyday life. Therefore, swadhyaya should not be given up even for a single day by a sadhaka, no matter how evolved he may be.

Learn a lesson from the illustrious examples of great sages. Be forever a sadhaka, an aspirant thirsting after spiritual knowledge, a student, eager to listen to the stories of the Lord or to spiritual discourses. Preserve within the youthful zeal and devout eagerness to practise sadhana and to realize more deeply the inexhaustible spiritual truth extolled and expounded by the saints, sages and seers from time immemorial.

How many sublime thoughts are brought to one's very door by the scriptures. Study carefully and systematically the *Bhagavad Gita*, *Ramayana*, *Srimad Bhagavatam*, *Vishnu Sahasranama*, *Lalita Sahasranama*, *Aditya Hridaya*, the *Upanishads*, *Yoga Vasishtha*, the *Bible*, *Zend Avesta*, the *Koran*, the *Tripitakas*, the *Guru Granth Sahib*, etc. Underline the sentences that have a direct bearing on one's life. Reflect on them in moments of leisure. Read and re-read the same spiritual sentences over and over again until they are indelibly engraved in the heart, and practise them in action until they become part and parcel of everyday behaviour.

Swadhyaya is also introspection and self-analysis. Be cautious, vigilant and circumspect. Watching the mind is introspection. One in a million does this beneficial, soul-elevating practice or discipline. People are immersed in worldliness and have no time to think of the soul or higher spiritual matters. The sun dawns, the mind runs in its usual sensual grooves of eating, drinking, amusement and sleeping. The day has

46

passed. In this way the whole life passes away. There is neither moral development nor spiritual progress.

Daily self-analysis and self-examination is an essential aspect of swadhyaya sadhana. Only then can the sadhaka obviate his defects and progress in sadhana. A gardener watches the young plants very carefully, removes the weeds daily, erects a strong fence round them and waters them daily at the proper time. Only then do they grow beautifully and yield fruits quickly. In the same way, the sadhaka should find out his defects through daily self-analysis and then eradicate them through suitable means. If one method fails, he must take recourse to a combined method of prayer satsang, pranayama, meditation, dietary regulation, self-enquiry, and so on.

Not only do the big waves of pride, hypocrisy, passion, anger, etc. that manifest on the surface of the conscious mind need to be eradicated, but also their subtle impressions that lurk in the corners of the subconscious mind. Only then is the sadhaka safe. These subtle impressions are very dangerous, lurking like thieves and attacking the aspirant when he is a bit careless, when he slackens his daily spiritual practices a bit and when he is provoked. If these defects do not manifest even under extreme provocation on many occasions, even when one is not practising daily introspection and self-analysis, rest assured that the subtle impressions also are obliterated.

The practice of swadhyaya through introspection and self-analysis demands patience, perseverance, tenacity, application, iron determination, subtle intellect and courage, but will yield a fruit of incalculable value. That fruit is immortality, supreme peace and infinite bliss. The sadhaka will have to pay a heavy price for this. Therefore, do not grumble when practising this aspect of sadhana every day. Rather, apply the mind, heart, intellect and soul fully to this sadhana.

Spiritual diary
Maintaining a spiritual diary is an indispensable requisite for the spiritual aspirant treading the path to realize God. It is a whip to goad the mind towards righteousness and God. It

is one's guru, teacher and guide. It provides solace, satisfaction and peace of mind. The aspirant who maintains a diary is happy for he is very close to God.

The aspirant should record in the spiritual diary the time of getting up in the morning, the time of retiring, the number of hours spent in sleep, the time given to studying the scriptures, the number of malas of japa done each day, the amount of time given to meditation, the nature of mistakes made during the day, the number of times anger arose and how long it lasted, the number of hours spent in selfless service, the number of times passion was a problem, the amount of time spent in asana and pranayama practice, the time wasted in useless company and idle gossip, the amount of time spent in mouna daily, the progress made in developing virtues, how often bad habits were not controlled, which sense organ was the most troublesome, and so on.

The spiritual diary will help the aspirant to evolve quickly. There is no better friend or more faithful teacher or guru. If the diary is kept properly, it will teach the value of time and how easily it slips away. It will check the happy-go-lucky ways of the mind and eventually destroy them. Be perfectly honest when filling in the diary, for it is for one's own benefit and progress. It is the diary of a spiritual aspirant who is treading the path of truth to realize God. Accept faults openly and try to rectify them. Record every detail in the diary. It is helpful to compare the progress of the present week with that of the previous one, or if unable to do this, compare the present month with the previous one, and make any necessary adjustments.

Regularity and punctuality are very important in daily sadhana. If one is careless and discontinues the practice or loses enthusiasm, it will be very difficult to revert to it again. The mind has the habit of sliding downwards. It is really an uphill task to compel the mind to move towards discipline and spiritual practices. Aspirants generally begin their practices with great zeal and enthusiasm, but after some time, due to slackness, they lose interest and begin to falter, often giving up sadhana altogether. This is not desirable. By means of the spiritual diary keep a close watch and see what progress is being made. Maintaining a spiritual diary will give a clear idea of the sadhana that is to be done and the mistakes that have been made during a particular period. It will serve as a check. Blessed is the aspirant who keeps a diary and reviews it regularly.

Grace

However strong the individual efforts may be, it is impossible to eradicate the *vrittis*, subtle modifications of the mind, the subtle forms of lust, anger, jealousy, delusion, pride, etc. One may do sadhana for thousands of lives and yet, without the grace of the Lord, one will not be able to burn the roots of the thought patterns lurking in the corners of the mind from time immemorial. God selects or chooses that aspirant whom He wishes to elevate and liberate. The *Kathopanishad* says, "Not by spiritual discourses, not by intelligence, not by study of many scriptures is this atman is attained; that man who is chosen by the Lord attains the Supreme."

All that happens has His essence as the basis. He has His own reasons for bringing everything about. Do not identify with anything. The Lord's grace will do everything, but remember that God helps those who help themselves. God's grace will descend only on those who make continuous effort to practise sadhana. The more one surrenders, the more one experiences grace at every step. Be up and doing. Give everything of oneself. Plunge into the sadhana of selfless service. The Lord will shower His grace, as He did for Mira, who abandoned everything. She renounced kingdom, husband, relatives, friends and property. She remembered her Lord Krishna all day and night. She shed tears of divine love. She sang His praises with single-minded devotion. Her mind was ever absorbed in Lord Krishna and He showered His grace upon her.

Surrender and grace are interrelated. Surrender draws down grace and grace makes surrender complete. Surrender

49

starts the purification of the heart, and grace completes it. Without grace, complete unification is not possible. Grace divinizes one's being in order that the inspiration to practise sadhana can be received and retained. Surrender is not something that happens in a week or a month. The aspirant cannot surrender totally from the very beginning of his sadhana, for the very purpose of sadhana is to be able to surrender totally to the will of the divine, to be one with the highest consciousness and receive His grace by becoming a divine instrument in the service of humanity. The desire for liberation alone makes one fit to develop devotion and receive God's grace.

Release all energies for a higher purpose, for spiritual attainment. Practise self-restraint and selflessness. Practise the sadhana of *bhakti yoga*, supreme devotion and intense attachment to the Lord through the nine modes of bhakti: *shravana*, hearing the lilas of the Lord; *kirtan*, singing His praises; *smarana*, remembering God's name; *padaseva*, worshipping the lotus feet of God through serving humanity and the poor; *archana*, offering of flowers; *vandana*, prostration and prayer; *dasya*, being the servant of the Lord; *sakhya*, being the friend of the Lord; and *atma nivedan*, identifying with the Supreme in complete self-surrender. The Lord's grace descends in proportion to the degree of the aspirant's surrender.

5

Overcoming Obstacles in Sadhana

Once the aspirant actually makes up his mind and starts regular sadhana, he may be assailed by a host of difficulties and problems that were not there before. At the start obstacles may beset the aspirant on every side and he will begin to think that commencing sadhana started all the trouble and he was better off before. However, do not be dismayed, as there is a reason for it. Sadhana implies imposing certain restrictions or disciplines, whereas previously the aspirant had always followed the course of the senses and therefore never had any opposition from them.

However, the path of the spiritual aspirant lies through a bewildering jungle of difficulties and dilemmas, problems and paradoxes. When sadhana is started, these complications will arise. One vexing paradox is that the mind is both one's best friend and one's bitter enemy. The mind becomes a true friend only after being gradually trained to be so. The mind begins to be really helpful after the aspirant has made sufficient progress in spiritual sadhana. Until then it should be regarded as a troublesome and untrustworthy antagonist within. It is extremely subtle, cunning and crooked, it is an arch deceiver.

When sadhana becomes an uphill task

One of the master strokes of the mind's artfulness is to make the aspirant feel and smugly imagine that he knows his mind

51

perfectly well and cannot be led away by it, while at the same time it will delude him totally. The mind has the knack of making the unwary aspirant confidently think he is the master, while it makes a hopeless fool of him. Therefore, managing the mind is the main practice of sadhana. Only through introspection, analysis, discrimination, vigilance and prayer can the subtle jugglery of this wonderful thing called the mind be understood and its deceptions and tricks transcended.

In the beginning, the path of sadhana is primarily one of both external and internal discipline, which means coming into conflict with the unruly, self-willed sense propensities of one's character. The aspirant begins to feel their force, whereas formerly they seemed to be comparatively quiet or non existent. This is what happens when sadhana is taken up in earnest.

As sadhana progresses, it can become a regular uphill battle against the entire current of age-old worldly tendencies. It means regaining the height that was lost in the unchecked downward descent into the abyss of gross worldliness. The beginner is quite unused to this struggle, effort and strain. Such a concerted deluge of troubles and difficulties confuses and unnerves him for a time. This is natural, so do not be perturbed. Bear these initial difficulties with fortitude, and they will soon vanish. Strength will be gained day by day. If the aspirant considers the troubles, trials and risks that are ordinarily borne in worldly matters, such as a monetary gain, a business deal, an examination or lawsuit, then he will readily endure all the early difficulties faced upon entering the path of sadhana. Always bear in mind the infinite, immeasurable and imperishable spiritual treasure that will ultimately be attained.

Trials and difficulties strengthen the aspirant

All sorts of obstacles come in the way of sadhana. Disappointment, despair, sickness, irritability, depression, doubt, indecision, lack of physical and mental energy, slothfulness, physical unsteadiness and craving for sensual objects all act

as stumbling blocks. During these trials and difficulties in sadhana the aspirant may begin to feel utterly helpless, but always remember that hope and help will come from within if there is unshaken faith in God. Never be discouraged. Always remember that there can be no strength or success without suffering and that no one is free from pain, disease, troubles and difficulties. Without sorrows, without persecution, no one can become a saint or a sage.

All suffering is meant for upliftment and development. It is the means of evolving potentialities and seeking a higher level of consciousness or existence. Suffering augments the powers of endurance, mercy and faith in a higher reality and removes egoism. Suffering purifies the soul, burning up gross material sins and impurities. It gives inner spiritual strength and develops willpower. Hence sufferings are blessings in disguise.

The aspirant will have to be very careful. Every time he becomes a victim of a passion or a problem of any kind, it is a little more difficult to resist its next attack. However, success in the attempt to subdue the problem will give the courage to resist it the next time it arises. Always keep a balanced mind. Irritability, for instance, manifests as an outburst of temper when any opportunity offers itself. Do not allow it to assume the form of a big wave of anger, but nip the irritability in the bud. Although difficult, this is a very important practice and will have to be done at any cost. Only then can real peace of mind be enjoyed.

Trials come to strengthen aspirants, so never be despondent. One will grow quickly if one can adapt to any kind of environment and circumstance. If God gives trials, side by side He also gives new strength, patience and fortitude to bear the trials. There is no reason to lament. Say once more, "Your will be done." All the saints and sages, prophets and seers had to pass through tremendous struggles and severe ordeals before reaching the goal.

Do one's best

During the practice of sadhana, the aspirant must be prepared to meet with hundreds of failures and obstacles. In the beginning sadhana may appear to be very hard, thorny, precipitous and slippery. It is like walking on the edge of a sharp razor. Do not brood over past mistakes and failures, as this will only fill the mind with grief, regret and depression. Be cautious and avoid repeating them. Just think of the causes which led to the failures and try to remove them in the future.

Great things have small beginnings and all growth is gradual. On the spiritual path there are constant setbacks. Repeated endeavour, constant vigilance and undaunted perseverance are needed. When desires are gradually thinned out, when the bonds of karma are gradually loosened and ignorance is dispelled, one will become more peaceful, strong and serene, and experience light from within.

Do not give up the struggle or the sadhana, despite repeated failures. Never be discouraged, but keep doing the best one can. If the aspirant is sincere and earnest in sadhana, he

54

will lift himself up quickly each time he falls and walk again with more zeal, boldness and cheerfulness. Success will come in the end. Slowly develop willpower. Every stumbling block will become a stepping stone to success or ascent of the hill of spiritual knowledge. Do not lose sight of the goal. Success is closer each time, so become firm and unshakeable.

There is immeasurable strength and power within, so do not be dejected. The Indweller will guide and raise one up. There is a glorious future waiting, so face all difficulties with a smile. Pain is the real eye-opener and the real guide. Understand that God puts one to severe tests to make one stronger and more powerful.

Continue with enthusiasm and joy
In the beginning the aspirant is very enthusiastic and gives sadhana a great deal of importance in his life. He expects to have some enlightening experiences and becomes discouraged if this does not happen. He then loses interest in the practices, slackens his efforts, loses faith in the efficacy of the sadhana and gives it up completely. This is a serious mistake.

Regular spiritual practice should never be given up under any circumstances. Drop all expectations. If the aspirant is sincere and devoted to his daily routine, meditation, selfless service and other practices, his sadhana will proceed according to the requirements of his soul. Sometimes the mind gets easily bored with one particular kind of sadhana and wants some new kind. Just as the mind wants variety in food and other things, so also it wants variety in the mode of sadhana and rebels against monotonous practice. At this stage the aspirant should learn how to go deeper into his practice and experience the subtleties that constantly arise. He needs to expand his vision of the purpose of sadhana.

It takes a long time to purify the mind and to become one-pointed. Practise sadhana regularly. It may take ten, twenty or thirty years or more of unbroken sadhana. It is a long, arduous path for the bravest of the brave. Always be positive and patient. Be careful in choosing companions, as undesirable people easily shake one's faith and belief. Continue sadhana with zeal and enthusiasm. The aspirant will have quick spiritual progress and ascend the spiritual ladder step by step and reach the ultimate goal.

Drop preconceived notions

Take up the practice of sadhana with an open mind. Then as one proceeds on the path, one will understand things gradually. Let go of pet notions and particular ways of responding and be free of preconceived notions formed by egoism. Approach the spiritual path with a sincere, receptive attitude to understand and learn through experiences, whatever they may be. Be prepared to adapt in order to overcome unforeseen events. Otherwise, disharmony will mark the very beginning of sadhana and this will taint the entire course of subsequent sadhana. Sadhana should be based on and supported by keen enthusiasm and joy.

The aspirant starts spiritual life with definite self-formed ideas about sadhana, realization, guru, and the like. But true spiritual life is often quite different from how it is imagined to be. All preconceived notions receive a rude shock. More often than not the beginner is unable to reconcile himself to these unexpected eye-openers and usually returns to his former deluded sensual life. This is a great mistake. A peerless gem is grasped in the hand and then foolishly thrown away. A priceless opportunity is lost. The mind will once again pursue the same sensual grooves as before, as the aspirant does not wish to let go of long-cherished conceptions which the ego clings to. He has, for instance, a certain idea of what constitutes sadhana and imagines that his guru will prescribe a sadhana to suit his ideas. When this does not happen, dissatisfaction begins.

Have full faith in the spiritual preceptor and the sadhana being pursued. To surrender at the feet of the guru and then begin to doubt or dislike his conduct is the biggest error an aspirant can ever commit. With this he severs the very root

56

of his sadhana and spiritual life. Such disillusionment and disappointment at the very start of spiritual life is a difficult handicap, which will cripple the capacity and urge for sadhana. The aspirant will lose heart and be disgusted with spiritual life.

The mind is *maya*, the play of illusion. The function of the mind is to veil the Truth and prevent even a glimpse of the highest reality. The aspirant has to be alert, therefore, and continuously counter its moves at every step. Be fully aware that when one seeks to enter the spiritual path, the mind will create all kinds of ideas of duty, responsibility, important undertakings, and so forth, which never troubled it before. There are different duties at different times, but doing sadhana for higher spiritual realization is the most important and urgent duty that is present throughout life right up to the last moment. The aspirant cannot afford to postpone or delay it even for one single moment.

Beware subtle forms of the lower nature

Self-sufficiency, arrogance, vanity, self-assertion and self-will are the constant companions of self-justification. Mark how maya influences deluded people! Maya tests sadhakas at every step and at every stage of their sadhana. The student who is a victim of self-sufficiency thinks foolishly that he knows everything. He is quite contented with his little knowledge and achievements and never attempts to acquire further knowledge. He stops his sadhana prematurely, foolishly thinking he has achieved the ultimate. He never endeavours to attain the highest knowledge of the highest Self. He does not know that there is a vast realm of knowledge beyond. He is like the toad in the well which has no knowledge of the ocean, and thinks that the well is the only illimitable expanse of water.

Self-sufficiency is a strong weapon of maya with which she deludes people and puts a strong brake on the sadhana of an aspirant. She does not allow him to proceed further or look beyond the veil, as he is carried away by false contentment. The self-sufficient yogic student who experiences transcendental sounds and flashes of lights thinks that there is nothing beyond this. The self-sufficient aspirant who knows the *Bhagavad Gita* and the Upanishads by heart thinks that there is nothing beyond this. The self-sufficient sadhaka who has experiences of lower samadhi thinks that there is nothing beyond this. All are groping in the dark and do not know what perfection is.

Self-justification is a very dangerous habit. The aspirant acts wrongly and tries to stick to his own ideas, own course of action and own position. He gives incorrect interpretations of the scriptures to support himself and will never admit his mistakes and faults. He tries to keep up his self-esteem and cannot perceive things in their true light. No one can help such a person. He cannot make any progress in sadhana as he will not listen to the instructions of elders or sages.

A self-assertive nature is a great obstacle on the spiritual path. It is a quality born of rajas, accompanied by vanity and arrogance. The aspirant who is a slave of the self-assertive nature wants to cut an important figure. He poses as a great yogi with many siddhis and says, "I am very advanced in sadhana. I can influence many people. I possess tremendous psychic powers." He expects others to pay their respects to him.

The self-assertive aspirant does not pay attention to the instructions of the guru, but pretends to be obedient to the guru. At every step the little ego asserts itself. Such an aspirant is disobedient and does not follow any discipline. He criticizes and has no faith in the scriptures and the words of sages. He may even insult his own guru. This type of aspirant who sticks tenaciously to his own foolish ideas cannot make any definite progress on the path of sadhana. Watch out for this aspect of human nature. Always be eager to receive good instructions from any source, from any sage. Be ever ready to grasp the truth.

Finally, the most dangerous deception played by the mind is in connection with sadhana itself. The very sadhana that is adopted by the aspirant to transfigure and divinize his life is converted into a prop and a field for the play of the ego and senses. It is very difficult to break out of this ensnaring net without the guidance of a higher soul. It is this attitude to sadhana that keeps the sadhaka stuck on the path, arresting progress for years together. For example, a youthful sadhaka with a sweet voice and musical talent naturally takes up kirtan and bhajan as his sadhana. He is in demand, becomes popular amongst devotees and the mind now spreads the net. His kirtans become sweeter day by day. New songs and tunes are added to his repertoire. Without his being aware, the kirtan has become a means to attract others and to maintain his popularity. Thus, the sadhana has developed a dual purpose: for God's darshan and side-by-side for worldly attraction. The result is the extraordinary phenomenon of the sadhaka caught in his sadhana; instead of liberation the quality of sadhana becomes bondage. Maya is wonderful, indescribable, her ways are mysterious and inscrutable.

Keep an open mind

The object of sadhana is to release life from the limitations with which it is bound. No sadhana ever goes in vain, as every bit is credited immediately towards one's evolution. Go on calmly with the sadhana and avoid thinking negative thoughts. Without missing a single day proceed onward with the spiritual practices. Little by little power will accumulate and grow. The fruit of sadhana cannot come immediately. Spiritual evolution is gradual and the aspirant will have to wait patiently for a long time, so do not become impatient.

Enter and travel along the path of sadhana with an open mind, free of all prejudices. Be fully aware of the onerous and indispensable purpose of sadhana and endure calmly and cheerfully all the trials and tests it offers. As one advances in sadhana and attains a greater and greater degree of evolution day by day, by regular and continuous practice, the clouds of doubt and delusion disperse by themselves. As the sun rises, the mist disappears. In the same way, as one progresses on the spiritual path by the grace of guru and God, all the intricate problems of life and death dissolve into the ever-abiding truth of existence. The sadhaka will inherit eternal life, everlasting splendour, peace and bliss!

6

Some Important Sadhanas

Easy sadhana in worldly environment

Due to the veil of ignorance people have forgotten their real essential nature, the sat-chit-ananda state. It is not at all necessary to renounce the world and run to some Himalayan cave to regain this lost divinity. There is an easy sadhana by which higher spiritual consciousness can definitely be attained, even while living in the world amidst multifarious activities. An aspirant need not necessarily have a separate meditation room or a fixed time for this practice, as it may be done whenever there is time available. The habit will come only by repeated practice.

Close the eyes for a minute or two once every two hours and think of God and His divine qualities, such as love, joy, knowledge, compassion, mercy, purity, perfection and so forth. Mentally repeat *Hari Om*, or *Sri Ram*, or *Ram Ram*, or any other mantra according to initiation or disposition. Feel all along that the body is a moving temple of God, that the office or business house is a big temple, and all activities such as walking, eating, breathing, seeing, hearing, reading and so on are offerings to the Lord. Work is worship, work is meditation, when done in the right spirit.

Work for work's sake without any motive, without the idea of agency, the feeling of 'I am the doer,' 'I am the enjoyer,' and without any expectation of fruits. Feel that one is an instrument in the hands of God and that He works through one's organs. Feel also that this world is a manifestation of the Lord and that children, husband, wife, father, mother and other relations are the images or children of the Lord. See God in every face and in every object. If this changed angle of vision and divine *bhava* or feeling is developed by protracted and constant practice, all actions will become *pooja*, worship of the Lord. This is quite sufficient. Higher spiritual realization will come soon.

This is a dynamic yoga sadhana. It is an easy sadhana, so no longer have the old lame excuse that there is no time to do spiritual practices. Even if this dynamic sadhana is practised for three months, one will become an entirely changed being. Realize right now one's identity and intimate relationship with all beings, with ants and dogs, elephants and tigers, Muslims and Hindus, Jews and Christians. There is only a degree of difference in manifestation or expression.

All forms belong to God or *saguna Brahman*, the Lord with qualities or attributes. When looking at a tree or a shrub, a Sikh or a Christian, endeavour to behold the real hidden consciousness behind the veil of form. Doing this for some time will lead to a feeling of inexpressible joy. All hatred will cease. Cosmic love or unity of consciousness will develop. This will be a magnanimous experience.

Here are some mantras for effecting ungrudging and total self-surrender. Repeat them mentally several times daily with bhava and contemplate their meaning: "O Lord, I am Yours, All is Yours. Your Will be done. You are everything." This practice will remove egoism and mineness and also the idea of being the doer.

For half an hour daily, write the ishta mantra in a notebook, observing mouna and without turning to this side or that. Write down in bold type on slips of paper: 'Speak the truth'; 'Om courage'; 'Om purity'; 'I must realize God'; 'Time is most precious'; 'I am an embodiment of courage, purity, mercy, love and patience'. Place them in the bedroom, dining room, living room, kitchen and veranda. Also keep some slips in the pocket and diary. This is an easy sadhana for developing virtuous, divine qualities.

Collective sadhana

There is peculiar *shanti*, peace, and *ananda*, bliss, in collective sadhana. Even if there are only six participants, collective sadhana must be done. The members will have special enthusiasm and interest in collective sadhana, otherwise individually they are likely to be overpowered by sleep and inertia, laziness and procrastination. Collective sadhana such as meditation, prayer, sankirtan, likhit japa and akhanda kirtan in groups, reading the *Bhagavad Gita* or the *Ramayana*, and so forth are more potent or effective than individual meditation, kirtan or individual sadhana. When people join together and practise meditation or sankirtan, everyone receives the combined effect produced by the simultaneous efforts of all those taking part in the common spiritual sadhana.

A large number of people generate and send out a huge thought form. A corresponding large amount of spiritual energy flows in and stimulates the spiritual faculties of those who take part in the group function. The greater the number of participants, the greater the thought forms, the greater the flow of inward spiritual faculties. Spiritual entities, nitya siddhas, are present in those places where group spiritual functions are conducted. Like attracts like; this is the divine law. Rishis and yogis transmit their vibrations to such places. Those who have inner sight can directly behold the spiritual vibratory lines of communication.

Furthermore, the simultaneous effort wonderfully harmonizes the vibrations of their bodies and minds and consequently makes them more receptive. The five *koshas* or sheaths vibrate rhythmically. When there is rhythm or harmony in the vehicles, meditation comes without any effort. The attention is focused or riveted on the same point. People think and feel together, in unison, and therefore stimulate one another.

Apart from daily collective sadhana, special sadhana programs should be carried out on a large scale on holidays or special occasions for three or more days. In Kali yuga such spiritual gatherings are maha yajnas. The main object of these collective sadhanas is to create a spiritual awakening in those people who are carried away by materialistic influences, who have forgotten all about their divine nature. These sadhanas also reinforce the spiritual attitude that has already awakened in those who are leading a spiritual life while living in the world.

When many people join together and practise common sadhana, a huge spiritual current of maha shakti is generated. This purifies the hearts of the practitioners and the atmosphere elevates them to the sublime heights of divine ecstasy. Common sadhana has this particular advantage. These magnanimous and powerful soothing vibrations are carried away to distant places. They elevate the mind, bring solace, strength and peace to all people and work as invisible harbingers of peace and harmony.

Further, the people are benefited by the valuable discourses and spiritual instructions given by sannyasins, yogis and other learned persons who are present on the occasion. Spiritual conferences tend to produce lasting unity and love amongst people. The spiritual waves can cure diseases and a host of other ailments, overhaul worldly samskaras, change the nature of rank materialists and confirmed sceptics, and infuse an uplifting spirit in the delegates.

Therefore, all spiritually inclined persons should try their level best to attend collective sadhana programs in different centres, towns, cities and countries. Meet together, meditate together, with a like mind, a united heart and a united intention. May there be welfare in the whole world. May all beings devote themselves to doing good to others.

Mouna sadhana
Mouna is silence. It is absolutely necessary for a spiritual life. Much energy is wasted by idle gossiping and tall talk. Mouna conserves energy, develops willpower and controls

64

the impulses of speech. With regular practice the energy of speech will be sublimated into spiritual energy and utilized for other practices of sadhana.

Controlling the speech is *karana mouna*. When the senses are silent, it is termed *indriya mouna*. The complete cessation of physical actions while observing silence is *kashtha mouna*. In kashtha mouna, one should not make any gestures, write anything or express ideas in any manner. In deep slumber there is *sushupti mouna*. However, perfected mouna comes only when duality and separation are absent, when all mental modifications or vrittis cease. This is maha mouna or para brahman.

The *vak indriya*, organ of speech, is a strong weapon of maya to delude aspirants and distract their minds. Quarrels and disputes occur through the play or mischief of this turbulent sense. If this sense is controlled, half the mind is already controlled. The tongue must be controlled steadily and gradually. In the beginning it will try to rebound. Be courageous. Do not allow anything to come out from the mind through the organ of speech. Observing silence and thinking of God or Brahman in earnest will help.

Vak mouna, remaining silent, is a great help for every beginner in sadhana. Even sadhakas practising advanced sadhana should practise vak mouna. They should not be puffed up with false egoism and pride, thinking that there is no necessity for this practice. One should clearly understand the value of mouna and feel that much benefit will be derived from practising it. Understand that by observing mouna, much peace, inner strength and joy will be experienced. Only then will there be pleasure in observing mouna and will one attempt to speak only when necessary. Forced mouna, simply to imitate or from compulsion, will make a person restless and gloomy.

In mouna sadhana, the sadhaka should keep fully occupied in japa, meditation or mantra writing. Introspect and practise self-analysis, watch the thoughts and begin to understand the ways of the mind and its workings. Notice how the mind runs from one object to another in a moment's time. If mixing with others while practising mouna, watch the mind whenever possible. Immense benefit will be derived from the practice of mouna. Real mouna is silence of the mind. Physical mouna will eventually lead to silence of the mind. Only then will serenity, calmness, peace and inner spiritual strength be enjoyed.

Mouna sadhana develops willpower and checks the force of desire. It is a great help in observing truthfulness and controlling anger. Emotions are controlled and irritability is checked. Whenever there is irritability, stop all conversation and observe mouna. A practitioner of mouna will use measured words and his speech will be very impressive. In ordinary people there is not a bit of control over speech. They speak whatever they like at random, and are unable to check the current of speech. Observe mouna during times of illness. Energy is wasted in idle talking. Mouna conserves energy, exercises a marvellous, soothing influence on the brain and nerves, and will assist the healing processes.

Observe silence as a sadhana practice for at least one hour a day and one day a week, just as Mahatma Gandhi did. If circumstances prevent one from observing mouna, strictly avoid long talk, big talk, tall talk, all unnecessary talk, all sorts of vain debates and discussions. Observe mouna while eating. During the period of mouna do not make any gestures or other sorts of movements of the hands or body, as this is tantamount to talking. If anything is absolutely necessary, write it on a piece of paper. If not in a position to practise properly, it is better to leave mouna until one is fully prepared to undertake it. Busy people can adopt a short sadhana of mouna at least for half an hour daily for their own spiritual growth.

Observe mouna at any convenient time in the morning or evening, besides the hours of silence spent in meditation. Try to become a sadhaka of measured words. This is itself mouna. To talk profusely for six months and to observe mouna for six months is of no benefit. The mind will be waiting to hurl the aspirant down into the deep abyss of ignorance whenever it gets an opportunity. Therefore, be very careful and vigilant.

For a beginner or an average aspirant, mouna sadhana for a protracted period does more harm than good. Instead be regular in the daily sadhana. Mouna for a few days or even one week will be of immense help for aspirants in order to manage the tongue and study the movements of the mind. When keeping mouna for a day or a week, utilize as much time as possible in japa and meditation. May the aspirant attain peace through silence. May one enter into the stupendous ocean of silence through mouna sadhana. May one become a maha muni or a jivanmukta through mouna.

Yoga sadhana for health

Most diseases have their origin in overeating, sexual excess and outbursts of anger and hatred. Energy is depleted by fits of anger, so do not fret and fume. Develop the powers of endurance and resistance. The cells and tissues of the body are filled with poisonous materials when a person loses his temper and entertains deep hatred. If the mind is kept cool and calm at all times, there will be wonderful health, strength and vitality.

Strengthen the body, mind and nerves. Take plenty of exercise in the open air, substantial nutritious food, medicated oil baths and plenty of rest. Have both mental and physical recreation. Lead a well-regulated life. Be moderate in eating, drinking and enjoyments. Lead a spiritual life where all activities are a means for personal upliftment. All diseases will leave the body by themselves. All microbes will die when vitality, vigour and strength are at a flood tide. This is the secret of health and happiness.

Practising asana, pranayama, concentration and meditation regularly is the ideal treatment. Thinking too much about the disease and the body will only intensify the malady. It is very important to keep the mind fully occupied in some way or other. Take the mind away from the body and think of the diseaseless atma or soul within, the bedrock or substratum of the body and mind. Cultivate this kind of spiritual reflection and attain the painless state or immortal Brahman. Always have a cheerful countenance. Smile and laugh. Never forget that one is the bodiless, undying soul.

Get up at four and practise japa of Om or the guru mantra and also a short meditation practice. Meditate on Om. Think of Om. Sing Om. Om is ones' real name. Om is the best tonic, anchor, panacea or cure-all, 'pick-me-up' or sovereign remedy for all diseases. The name of the Lord is the best medicine in the world. Have intense faith in the power of the names of the Lord. Incurable diseases are cured by japa or singing Hari's name. Meditation creates new, healthy vibrations in all the cells of the body and removes disease. All the tissues are bathed in the nectar that flows during meditation. All the germs that cause disease are destroyed. The rationale of this kind of yogic or spiritual treatment is yet unknown to the medical profession.

Expose the body to the gentle rays of the sun for a short time daily in the early morning. The sun is the source of energy and power. Soak twelve almonds at night. Remove the skin and take the almonds with some sugar candy in the early morning, or make a refreshing beverage by grinding the almonds with a little black pepper and sugar candy. This is a fine, cooling and strength-giving tonic.

Rest in bed if necessary. Adjust the diet. Take simple, wholesome, easily digestible, bland and non-irritating food. Give up hot, pungent curries, chutneys and chillies. Rest the stomach and bowels by partial fasting. Fasting for a whole day is all the better. Fasting eliminates poisons and overhauls the system thoroughly. Take sago and milk, barley water and fruits like sweet oranges, grapes and so on. If thirsty, take lemon or orange juice with sugar candy. May God bless all with perfect health, a high standard of vigour, strength, vitality and longevity.

Brahmacharya sadhana

Brahmacharya means not only control of the reproductive organ, but also control of the senses and purity in thought, word and deed. In a narrow sense, brahmacharya is celibacy.

In the broad sense, it is absolute control of all the senses. Freedom from sensual thoughts in the waking as well as the dreaming states is perfected brahmacharya; the very idea of sensual enjoyment does not enter the mind. It is a potent weapon for controlling the internal rajasic forces of desire, anger, infatuation, and so on.

Brahmacharya is a fundamental qualification for an aspiring sadhaka. It is a most important virtue for self-realization, and higher spiritual progress is not possible without it. By correctly practising brahmacharya sadhana, the semen or ovum becomes transmuted into *ojas shakti*, vitality, and spiritual and intellectual power will increase, and can be used for spiritual pursuits. The vital energy, *virya*, the essence of life, thought and intelligence is preserved. When preserved, virya serves as a master key to open the realms of divine bliss and to obtain all sorts of higher achievements in life.

The practice of brahmacharya has two aspects: abstention and observance. Abstention means that all lust in the mind must be overcome, not only gross enjoyment. Observance, the second aspect, is "dwelling on Brahman", which is the literal meaning. Dispassion towards lustful enjoyments is never possible unless the aspirant develops passion for the spiritual goal and tastes spiritual joy. Brahmacharya is the supreme practice in yoga sadhana emphasized by Lord Krishna in the *Bhagavad Gita*. He clearly states that the vow of brahmacharya is necessary for meditation (6:14). He teaches that brahmacharya is one of the austerities of the body, *sharira tapas* (17:14), and that we can kill this powerful enemy, passion, by observing brahmacharya (3:43).

Brahmacharya is the foundation on which the ladder of higher sadhana stands. If the sadhaka is not established in brahmacharya, if the mind is agitated by sensual thoughts and desires, he will not be able to reach the summit of the ladder of sadhana, the highest nirvikalpa samadhi. The whole being must be completely transmuted by entertaining sublime divine thoughts and practising regular meditation. Transmuting sensual desire is a very potent way to realize eternal bliss.

69

A raja yogi conquers passion and attains *kaivalya*, emancipation, through the practices of yama, niyama, asana, pranayama, pratyahara, dharana, dhyana and samadhi. A jnana yogi becomes pure through viveka (discrimination), vairagya (dispassion), vichara (self-enquiry), shama (tranquillity), dama (control of the senses) and titiksha (endurance). By practising siddhasana, sirshasana, sarvangasana, moola bandha, uddiyana bandha, maha mudra, yoga mudra and nauli, a hatha yogi transmutes seminal energy into ojas shakti. By practising the nine steps of bhakti (shravana, kirtan, smarana, padaseva, archana, vandana, sakhya, dasya, atma nivedana) and japa, a bhakta destroys the impurity of his mind and fixes it on God.

Get up at four. Have a cold bath. Render the will pure, strong and irresistible. Whenever desire is troubling, try to attain viveka by looking into the defects of sensual life. Cultivate vairagya towards sensual pleasures. Withdraw the mind from objects and centre it on the Lord. Change the mental attitude and avert sexual thoughts by sublime divine thoughts. See the atman as the underlying essence in all. All names and forms are unreal, like a shadow, water in a mirage, blueness in the sky. Anything that brings impure thoughts into the mind is bad company. Have constant satsang, as the magnetic aura and powerful thought currents of developed adepts have a tremendous influence on the mind.

Remember the pains of samsara. Have a strong desire for liberation. Develop the 'mother' feeling towards all women. This will decidedly help to destroy lust. Do not look at obscene pictures or speak vulgar words. Do not read anything that excites passion and produces undesirable sentiments in the heart. Give proper attention to diet and take wholesome sattwic food. Transmute the sexual energy into spiritual energy through selfless service, karma yoga. These are important methods for becoming a true brahmachari.

Without perfect brahmacharya, substantial spiritual progress cannot be had in sadhana. There are no half measures on the spiritual path. Control the body first, then purify the thoughts. Make a firm resolve. Practise purity in thought, word and deed. May the Lord give spiritual strength to practise sadhana.

Start sadhana now
Sadhana is the beginning of a new life, a life of expansion, glory and divine splendour. It is the road to peace, happiness, prosperity and immortality. Draw inspiration from sadhana to grow, expand and evolve. Build up all the positive qualities: fortitude, patience and courage, that are dormant within. Let life be a radiance of purity, now and forever. Purify the mind in the flame of devotion and wisdom. The sadhana by which the sages reach perfection is the path of Truth. There is no other way to freedom or emancipation. Neither art nor science, neither study nor erudition are needed for higher spiritual realization, only faith, purity and devotion. Faith, hope and love alone will vitalize the aspirant's sadhana. Tread the path of sadhana and realize, "I am the immortal Self."

Sadhana

From the teachings of Swami Satyananda Saraswati

7

The Vision of Sadhana

Sadhana is a highly developed science of evolution, containing a wide range of techniques which are limitless in their scope and application. There has to be a total understanding of sadhana and why it is practised. Sadhana is not practised because one is a swami or a sannyasin or a disciple, or for an ashram, but for the evolution of oneself and who one is. Therefore, sadhana is not the end, but the means.

In Sanskrit, *sadhana* means spiritual effort, not physical or mental effort. It is the effort made to open the doors beyond which there is enlightenment. The term sadhana is a collective name for all those techniques which are deliberately adopted to remove the imperfections of the personality. These may include hatha yoga, meditation, karma yoga, bhakti, self-introspection, kriya yoga or many other practices. In the *Yoga Sutras* (1:14), Sage Patanjali explains the meaning of sadhana as being perfectly fixed in spiritual effort, as continuous practice which becomes part of the personality or individual nature. After perfecting the practices of sadhana and achieving higher spiritual consciousness, the sadhaka must still operate in the realm of prakriti, maya or duality, the manifest world. Many saints and sages, prophets and avatars, in spite of total identification with the higher spirit, have moved and lived and acted among people in the world.

Sadhana is the effort one makes to identify with the joy and sorrow of everyone, to extend the horizons and rise above

75

the pettiness of life; this should be the aim of sadhana. Identification in this sense ceases to be personal. There should be emotional integration with everyone. Swami Sivananda taught me to identify with the mind of a thief, of a liar, of one who spoke ill of me. His advice was, "Put yourself in their position, then you will understand them better." If such an attitude can be developed, then one is not very far from yoga *siddhi* or perfection in yoga. To attain *siddhis*, psychic powers, is easy, but to understand the purpose of sadhana is very difficult.

Purpose of sadhana

Some think or declare that the purpose of sadhana it is to cure disease. Others believe it develops the mental faculties by increasing the ability to concentrate. The ultimate purpose of sadhana is concerned only with practical methods of unfolding and awakening the potential already existing in every person's being and transforming life into an expression of joy. Aspirants are asking the way to prepare for that evolutionary experience. How to know the self, how to achieve samadhi, how to have internal communion, how to reach the inner temple? The practice of sadhana is the way.

Human beings are not just static creatures born to eat, drink, live and die. Where have we come from and where are we going? As Lord Krishna said to Arjuna, "Many lives have gone by and many lives will come again because evolution is an unending process." Everything in this universe is evolving, right from matter to spirit. Matter is evolving and undergoing constant change even in the realm of physics. The mind is higher matter which is also undergoing a constant, natural and systematic transformation from age to age, from year to year.

A time will come when mind and matter will undergo an ultimate transformation into spirit. Matter is the base and within it lies a dormant energy. By the process of sadhana, the two elements in existence, consciousness and matter, are separated from each other. When matter, consciousness and energy are separated from each other, that is moksha, nirvana,

samadhi, shoonyata. That is the higher vision and it has to be materialized through the process of sadhana. Fundamental change is not brought about from outside; it is inherent in the material. The mind can be transformed into higher consciousness only because the potentiality or *atman*, the self beyond mind and body, is already present. Only ignorance, *avidya*, needs to be removed, and sadhana is the means to remove it.

Perceiving the highest truth

Sadhana is practised to attain a greater power and capacity in one's life, to directly perceive the highest truth, the highest potential. Pleasures that are fleeting and temporary are not the truth. The happiness one gets from the world is relative; it is dependent on friends, money and other things. However, there is a permanent state of experience called *ananda*, which is not ordinary happiness, but a permanent and unchanging state. Neither the body or mind are experienced; nothing

77

material is experienced. It is in the form of a sound or a transcendental feeling, or in the form of *shoonya*, the void, or in the form of a universal experience. Once that permanent state of mind has been attained, then nothing matters in life. It can be experienced only when one has experienced one's real self.

During that moment of experience, this individual is not there. That existence is beyond the psychological and emotional limitations normally experienced as 'I', body, name, place. That existence is known as transcendental experience, heaven, nectar, immortality, God, Truth. It is an experience. It is for this that all are striving in sadhana. Therefore, all one's sincerity must be directed to this purpose. In order to have direct knowledge of God, one must plunge into yoga sadhana. Only then will He be realized as the creator as well as the 'soul and stuff' of creation.

Sadhana in daily life

Sadhana is no longer confined to mysticism and philosophy. It is the practical application of the techniques in one's daily life. Sadhana does not have any preconceived axioms or philosophy. It can be practised by those who believe in religion and those who do not, by those who believe in morality and those who do not, and by those who believe in higher spiritual life and those who do not. Originally sadhana was meant to liberate mankind from the pain of bondage, but over time it became the creed of a select few. Now, however, this has changed and sadhana needs to be understood in the context of one's own life.

Human life is most blessed as it is a signal indicating the beginning and growth of the divine life within. In animal life, we are compelled to learn the use and control of limbs and forms. In human life, man learns the use and control of the mind and develops latent mental powers to the extreme. Through sadhana the hidden powers of the mind are unearthed which can be utilized for successful living and for spiritual realization.

Overcoming limitations

Everywhere in the world people are suffering. Every individual feels imprisoned within, defeated, dumbfounded, oppressed and bewildered. The biggest enemy is one's own limitations. In the ancient literature these limitations were referred to as evil forces, devils and demons. The practice of spiritual sadhana frees one from this feeling of defeat and bewilderment.

Only during the period of sadhana is one wholly immersed in the process of delving deep within. At other times the awareness is externalized, but during sadhana the passage of time is momentarily transcended and the infinite borders of space are crossed. One exists unseen, unknown, yet one's existence is a total reality. At that moment, one is able to experience an abstract facet of oneself, which in ordinary life is regarded as a myth.

Karmas are quick to accumulate. Samskaras are continually building up, which determine the future karma. Therefore, in order to counteract this constant inflow of impressions, one has to consistently follow some spiritual practice so that one does not become overburdened and bend with the weight. During the period of sadhana, the thoughts, passions, desires and other karma are expended at the subtle and causal levels and one emerges cleansed of many impurities and obstructions. That is precisely why one feels refreshed and light after an hour of spiritual practice, because part of the burden that has been carried for many decades in the different realms of consciousness has decreased. It is like shedding a heavy weight and releasing the tension.

Through sadhana, equanimity, serenity, one-pointedness of mind and strong determination are acquired. Lost confidence is regained. All these qualities are essential for successful living in all spheres of life, provided one knows how to utilize the energies generated by sadhana. So the aim of sadhana should be to acquire knowledge, dispassion, devotion, power and peace. If one fails to develop these through sadhana, one has missed the way.

79

Sadhana opens the inner chamber

An aspirant may want to become a yogi or yogini without yoga sadhana, but it is impossible to pass the examination without study. To achieve the highest aim of sadhana every bit of the personality should be transformed into awareness of the divine so that higher existence is expressed through the mind and senses while interacting in the world. Sadhana needs to be practised whereby all the ideals, sentiments and aspirations are changed, the speech, perceptions and conduct transformed.

The tenor and conduct of life must be changed. Turn the senses inwards. Make the mind quiet. Stop distractions. Be steady and immovable like Buddha. Practise self-enquiry: who am I, where am I and why? This is sadhana. Resort to Truth, not to the transience of the body and mind. Close the eyes and try to see afar. Close the gates and open the inner chamber. This truth can only be realized through years of protracted sadhana.

No one can realize the Supreme Being through the physical eyes, no one can hear the divine music while concerned with worldly tumults. It is only after the external perceptions have been withdrawn and the last traces of lower love and passion have also diminished that He comes, sings, loves and makes one blessed.

Try to make life eternally divine through the process of sadhana. Whenever there is time, go to satsangs and gradually learn the art of assimilating the wisdom of the sages. Encourage friends and neighbours to tread the path of Truth and lead a divine life. Read yogic and vedantic literature, reflect on it and implement whatever is possible in daily life. Practise asana, pranayama, mantra japa and sing kirtan. Become equipped with good speech, good health and a sound education. In this way, one will be able to serve people in a better way. One must have the strength to stand on ones' own feet. Every moment of life must be dedicated to higher ideals. Think twice or even more before putting a step forward. This is practical sadhana.

Sadhana includes everyone and everything

The world is full of selfishness, but the path of spiritual sadhana should not and cannot be selfish. Though one may be treading the spiritual path as an individual, it really includes everyone and everything else. If spiritual awakening is being sought for purely personal motives, this is an immediate block. It is like trying to be part of a family, or a member of a club, or working in an office, without the slightest consideration for others. It cannot be done. One can only be a perfect and integrated member of a family by harmonizing one's inner being and simultaneously having concern for other members of the family. It is the same with sadhana; when done for personal motives it is immediately self-defeating. There has to be the aspiration for self-perfection combined with interest in the welfare of all other people and things. There has to be regard for oneself and others. This is the essential balance required for success in sadhana. It implies equanimity in all spheres of being. Therefore, one should not merely practise sadhana but also live the divine life. A harmonious pattern should be created in one's whole life.

Higher dimensions

These teachings are to inspire aspirants to take their sadhana into a higher dimension, to merge the external with the internal and to make the consciousness infinite. While continuing with the sadhana, penetrate the external covering and open the inner gate. When the inner eye is opened, then one's higher self is seen. The ultimate truth has to be realized for oneself.

Rest assured one will be given what one aspires for. Do not land the soul in mad thinking. Just do sadhana and materialize the higher awareness, nothing more. Empty oneself. Tune the radio. Unite the mind. The rest will take place at the proper time. Perfect happiness is experienced only after having engaged in introspection and self-analysis, and then taken to the path of sadhana, determined to lead a virtuous and divine life.

Every action has three objectives: production, perfection and pleasure. To achieve perfection, man should do sadhana. If the sadhana cannot enrich one's present existence with beauty and health, success and gold, kick it off. Anything in spiritual life only for the life hereafter is not wanted. If the sadhana cannot bestow peace on the soul of this body, dash it off. Practise sadhana to know Him. Dedicate all actions to Him.

If one is inspired to take up sadhana and discover spiritual life, be assured that this aspiration has not just dropped from heaven. It is a culmination of the whole process undergone in life, all that has been both desirable and undesirable. This process is both internal and external. Internal means the mental, emotional and psychic aspects; external means the physical, social and economic aspects. Everything in existence should be considered as a part of the whole process of evolution. The spiritual aspirations one is exhibiting today are the sum total of what one has gone through in the past. It has not just come up from anywhere; it is an outcome of that totality.

Nivritti or pravritti sadhana
There are two main paths to realize the higher reality: pravritti and nivritti. Therefore, an aspirant must walk upon the path of life with perfect awareness of his spiritual destiny. The sadhana one chooses to practise depends on what attracts one's entire attention.

Pravritti is the path of spiritual evolution by involvement in desires, ambitions, emotions and all the *vrittis*, modifications of the mind, without renouncing any aspect of worldly life. The path of pravritti or involvement is not for sensual pleasure and enjoyments. Sensual life is a by-product. The real purpose is illumination, but it is a path which takes a long time. It is circuitous and not dangerous.

Nivritti is the path of total retirement from the vrittis, worldly life and society. Nivritti is an attitude of being ever aware of the goal, which is *moksha*, liberation. Nivritti marga is very difficult and even precipitous, but it is short.

The *Bhagavad Gita* makes it quite clear that the ultimate reality can be reached either by pravritti or nivritti. Pravritti or involvement is described in terms of *karma* or action and expression. Nivritti is the path of Samkhya, or awareness and experience. Some authorities contend that the supreme or ultimate reality cannot be attained by active involvement (pravritti), but can only be experienced through passive awareness (nivritti). However, the *Bhagavad Gita* clearly states that those who work and those who renounce will both reach that end, provided they resign their ego, surrender their lower self, purify their mind and discipline their senses. Householders can reach the higher path by detaching from or renouncing the idea of doership.

Karma sannyasa is the path of pravritti, or involvement. Sannyasa is the path of nivritti, or non-involvement. Sannyasa initiation is for those who have chosen to dedicate their lives to the search for the highest truth through the path of total surrender to the guru. The disciple renounces all personal ambitions, desires and attachments, completely dedicating himself to the service of his guru. The guru then uncovers the inherent potential within the disciple and after training him in the ashram, sends him far and wide to carry out his mission. Through personal sadhana and dedication to guru, the sannyasin evolves and in time serves as a guiding light to others.

Sannyasa initiation symbolizes the death of the disciple's previous identity and the birth of the new spiritual being. The sannyasin is born again in the same physical body. As a newly born sannyasin, he makes a promise to himself that he will always place his spiritual goal first and foremost in his life.

Four groups of sadhakas

Temperamentally, *sadhakas*, those who practise sadhana, can be classified into four groups: dynamic, emotional, mystical and rational. No one is purely dynamic or emotional or mystical or rational. Some are predominantly dynamic but have emotions, mysticism and rationality. They must take up karma yoga as the primary sadhana, as the main spiritual practice, but also utilize bhakti yoga, raja yoga and jnana yoga.

Those who are predominantly emotional must accept bhakti yoga, the yoga of devotion and love, as their main sadhana and along with that practise a little karma yoga, raja yoga and jnana yoga. Those who are predominantly mystical by temperament will have to accept and practise raja yoga sadhana, the yoga of meditation, concentration, contemplation and samadhi. But side by side, they will have to accept karma yoga, bhakti yoga and jnana yoga as part of their sadhana.

Each aspirant has to analyze his own temperament and accordingly accept one of the four sadhanas. Karma yoga is the yoga of action, work. Bhakti yoga is the yoga of devotion, singing, japa, prayer. Raja yoga is the yoga of meditation. Kundalini yoga, kriya yoga, laya yoga all come under the heading of raja yoga. Jnana yoga is contemplation, the yoga of thorough self-investigation.

Self-realization does not depend on sadhana

It needs to be understood that sadhana and self-realization are two completely different subjects. Self-realization cannot be reached by any yoga sadhana because it is not a distance; it is a state of consciousness which is here even now. Karma yoga, bhakti yoga, raja yoga or jnana yoga do not lead to self-realization. If one wants to go to Mumbai from Chennai, the train will take one to Mumbai, but if one has to go to America, that train will only lead one towards America. From Mumbai one will have to take a flight to Frankfurt, then another plane to London and a third flight to the destination. From the airport one will then have to travel to one's hotel by car or metro, and so on.

Sadhana proceeds in the same manner. Karma yoga purifies all levels of the mind; bhakti yoga eliminates distractions of the mind; jnana yoga removes *avidya*, ignorance; hatha yoga removes the possibility of suspension of mind, *laya avastha*; and raja yoga helps to integrate and concentrate the wandering tendencies of the mind. That is all. Even after these states have been attained, self-realization cannot be assured because these sadhanas are negative practices. I am using the word negative in a very positive sense. If I want to show a very important person around this room, first I will paint it, clean it and then make everything neat and tidy, so that the person fels at home when he comes. In the same way, these different paths of yoga sadhana purify the individual mind – but one must know how to get in.

The *Bhagavad Gita* states that no yoga or no way can lead directly to the point of self-realization. Why? Because all sadhanas belong to the realm of the mind, and the state of self-realization, atman, is not a mental state. How can a mental practice lead to a non-mental state? Sadhanas of jnana yoga, nada yoga, mantra, dharana and dhyana are practised through the mind. In the *Bhagavad Gita*, Lord Krishna tells Arjuna, "After you have practised yoga, after you have perfected yoga and reached a certain point of evolution, when the mind has been rendered subtle and pure, then I will give you buddhi yoga." Buddhi yoga is grace; it is a yoga which is in the form of enlightenment. It is not intellectual yoga, not intelligence or the normal buddhi through which right and wrong are known.

There is a higher point of termination in yoga sadhana, when a certain vision or revelation is given to the sadhaka. It is not due to sadhana. Sadhanas are necessary for the body, mind and emotions, for physical, emotional and mental balance, but no path reaches Him. All sadhanas are *bahiranga* or external, which have to be done because one belongs to the domain of the world. One has a body, a mind, a nervous system, so one has to practise asana and pranayama. Sadhanas clean the mirror so that its purity now reflects the light for one to see. With the experience of that enlightenment or an absolutely purified consciousness, there is oneness with the totality.

Sometimes there may be doubts, but never doubt that God gives darshan and can speak to the aspirant. Self-realization does not depend on the practices of sadhana. If it can be understood that sadhana and self-realization are two completely different subjects, and if one can convince oneself that even without sadhana self-realization can be had, then one will have it.

Spiritual awakening

People are becoming more and more aware of the need for spiritual life and sadhana, but they lack guidance, inspiration and the means of transmission. One point should be made clear. While a spiritual institution or philosophy or a religious institution or philosophy needs publicity and recognition, the awakening of spiritual consciousness in everybody, en masse, does not need any publicity at all. If guidance is needed in spiritual sadhana, it must be searched for. Let people remain seekers. Let seekers go to the gurus and teachers. Let them try different philosophies. Let them read books. I teach because people are searching for a way which will lead them towards the greater possibility which they have somehow realized in their mind. Since the 1960s the awakening has been marvellous and voluntary, in direct contrast to previous generations when there was no choice, and man was obliged to follow a path, whether he understood it or not.

True spiritual life is not an outcome of wild publicity or compelling or convincing people. Rather, it comes in a beautiful and concise way. If all the books and publicity were withdrawn and spiritual life was not propagated through newspapers, magazines or television, nevertheless the mass consciousness, which is trying to evolve spiritually, would discover its own way of sadhana. People of all ages are earnestly trying to discover a way for themselves, and this voluntary discovery of spiritual life and acceptance of spiritual practices is a very happy event. If this awakening continues and the voluntary efforts to raise spiritual consciousness are genuine and honest, then the sublime heights of consciousness can definitely be reached. People are searching for good books on yoga sadhana, for good yoga teachers and for good systems, and this is a very positive sign of awakening.

Sadhanas according to yuga

In each *yuga* or age there has been a particular part of the Vedas specifically allotted for the people of that age, to guide them in spiritual and worldly life. During Satya yuga, *dharma* or the 'right way of living' was given in the shrutis; during Treta yuga in the smritis; during Dwapara yuga in the puranas; and during Kali yuga in the agamas, nigamas and the sixty-four tantras. The sadhanas and the style of imparting spiritual knowledge in each of these scriptures pertain only to the people of that yuga. If the sadhana suited to one particular yuga is adopted in another yuga, it will not bear fruit because the capacity of the individual for faith and concentration changes from age to age.

In the *Maha Nirvana Tantra* it is said that if a person of Kali yuga performs the same yajnas or fire ceremonies that were formerly done in Satya yuga, their sadhana will not bear the desired fruit because of the absence of control of the animal instincts. Even today in Kali yuga, the spiritual knowledge and sadhanas given in the tantric texts can be understood by very few people. In this age people as a whole are unable to commit themselves to sadhana and the spiritual quest. They are more able to understand what they read in the newspapers. Nevertheless, they are collectively more attuned to the possibility of spiritual evolution through the practices of yoga, kirtan, chanting God's name, etc. than through austerities, conduct and observances which were most suitable for other ages and other generations of people.

The spiritual quest

The most important purpose in human life is the spiritual quest. All aspirants will have to make a shift from the superficial concept of the spiritual quest to the traditional, real concept. Sadhana for the evolution of the entire mass consciousness is the sadhana of the twenty-first century. Every individual has a mission, a purpose. If he has no purpose, the whole of creation, the whole of existence, all philosophy and all religions are completely baseless and purposeless. Living a life in total ignorance of its purpose is negating the philosophies, contradicting the religions. The means have become the purpose.

Therefore, at least once a day reflect on these questions: Why have I come? Why do I exist? What is my purpose? Am I the body? Am I this physical structure or is there a greater reality within me? How am I going to attune myself? Sadhana is practised to reach the highest stage of spiritual life and acquire self-knowledge, not because one is bound to one's guru by a promise. Surrender to the guru is not due to attachment, but because it constitutes one's support in order to reach the highest stage.

8

The Basis of Sadhana

Becoming established in sadhana

Many aspirants are very enthusiastic in the beginning, but their enthusiasm dwindles away later on. A spiritual aspirant must continue his sadhana until he is able to receive something very concrete and substantial. However, very few aspirants can do this. In spiritual life, twelve years is an important cycle, as many shastras say that sadhana takes that amount of time to begin to fructify. Consider that it takes many years for the body and mind to change. After a cycle of seven years all the body cells have been completely replaced, and it can be said one has a new body. However, it takes longer to restructure the mind and remould the awareness. Twelve years enables gradual and complete restructuring of the body, mind, emotions and psyche. Perhaps it takes that amount of constant sadhana to purify and prepare the pranic and psychic bodies for spiritual awakening.

It is also very important that sadhana be practised without interruption, with continuity, because if the practices are interrupted now and then, the student cannot receive their full benefit and cannot attain spiritual maturity. Sometimes people have the misconception that the task of spiritual evolution can be completed within a few months, but this is wrong. It may take many births to achieve. The aspirant should not be impatient; there should be no hurry or haste. The ancient

89

literature is full of stories wherein it is declared that it may take many births for an individual to attain the highest goal of sadhana.

What is important is not the length of time, but the fact that the practices have to be continued without any interruption and until the goal is achieved, whatever time it may take. One should not lose heart, but continue doing the practices with faith. Faith is the most important factor, for it is only through faith that there is the patience and energy to continue the practice against the odds of life. If the aspirant has complete faith in the fact that he will surely achieve the goal through his practices, then it matters little to him when he reaches the goal.

The next important point is that the aspirant should like sadhana to the highest extent. Just as a mother becomes disturbed if her child does not return home on time, so the aspirant should become disturbed if he does not do his daily practices. He should love his practices as much as he loves his body. He should be as attracted towards the practices as he is towards a sweet dish of his choice. The practices can produce the desired result only if they are done with love and attraction. There should be no feeling of compulsion, but the practices should be done willingly, with earnestness, respect and devotion. If a sadhaka has these qualities, good results are assured.

Faith in sadhana

If the aspirant is not fully convinced about his guru and God, there is absolutely no use in his sadhana. To succeed in sadhana an unshakeable faith and supreme love for the Lord have to be awakened in the heart. Faith presupposes love. Thus the object of faith is loved, then comes awareness, then merging, and finally realization. This is how sadhana progresses.

In the practice of sadhana, faith is the first and foremost requisite. Faith implies that one believes there is a good purpose for doing something. There has to be faith that the path of sadhana does lead to higher awareness and bliss, and will not lead into the depths of ignorance. Faith does not demand any proof or epistemological conclusions. Faith is an intuitive attitude. Though there may be lack of personal experience, one has sufficient faith to accept that the higher experience does exist. There has to be faith in the efficiency of the sadhana, otherwise one would never do anything.

Without faith no asanas, pranayama, meditative techniques or any other sadhana would be practised. When practice is translated into experience, then faith drops away; it becomes superfluous. Faith is associated with the instructions of the guru. Without faith one would not follow his instructions for sadhana.

Faith cannot be developed; it has to be realized. In order to realize and deepen faith, one must practise one's mantra, attend satsang more frequently and read the lives of great saints like Chaitanya, Mirabai, Dayananda and St Theresa. *Darshan*, meeting, with a great sage or one's guru will intensify faith, for one will see a living example of a person who has travelled the path that one is presently travelling. This is a great source of inspiration and intensifier of faith.

Faith gives stature to the personality and faith is power, strength; it is the wealth of the spiritual aspirant. One may be a great scholar who intellectually understands everything about sadhana, one may even practise sadhana day and night, visit the church or temple daily and have gurus and gurus, but without faith one will never see the inner self. Avidya, or ignorance, can only be eliminated by faith, which is made up of purity, simplicity and innocence. If by temperament an aspirant does not have faith in higher dimensions of consciousness, if he is not devotionally inclined, or is more intellectual and inclined towards the study of yoga, progress in sadhana is certain to be slow.

The secret of success in sadhana is to have the faith to dedicate oneself to highest sadhana. Only then can one aspire to attain higher virtues and live a divine life here on earth. This is a very important aid in keeping the faith in sadhana alive. As long as there is passion, anger, greed, delusion, fear, jealousy and egoism, one will not be able to exercise one's divine will. Again, so long as one has no guru, no mantra, no aim, no faith and no love or devotion, one will not be able to do away with dark forces that arise as sadhana progresses.

The heart which God has given should be given to the ideal. When it is given to desires, passions and sense pleasures, it causes restlessness and dissipation. When the same heart is given to a great ideal – union with the self in samadhi or self-realization – it experiences peace, attains power, perceives light and gains wisdom which can be utilized to benefit the entire creation. When the heart is given for sadhana, it becomes a link between divine and human, suprasensuous and sense experiences.

When I came to my guru, I was an atheist. As time passed and I practised yoga sadhana, I thought that in meditation one could only experience *shoonyata*, the void, and nothing else, just a blank. That was my ultimate philosophy. But my guru said, "No. The divine experience is not 'nothing'. It is a total experience, a complete experience. But to have this experience one must have love, devotion and faith in God."

Satsang

Satsang is one of the simplest and most effective means to aid the aspirant in the beginning of sadhana. In *satsang*, 'association with the truth', the 'true' existence is experienced. It is well-known that when associating with positive influences, one tends to develop in that direction. Satsang plays an important role in moulding the personality.

There is nothing as powerful as satsang for changing the thoughts, moods, sentiments and actions. The perception becomes clearer and the judgement more accurate. There will be a greater perception of one's limitations, strengths and weaknesses. Most important of all will be the realization of one's aim and goal of life. Reading sacred texts, dwelling on pious thoughts and thoughts about the atman, the company of saints, hearing devotional songs and divine stories are all various forms of satsang.

Attend satsang, discourses, talks and discussions on spiritual matters as much as possible. Look for people of great wisdom who can interpret the mysteries and fundamental truths of life as revealed through the scriptures, people who can inspire one to introspect and to question oneself positively. This practice of being in the company of wise and learned people can be incorporated into daily life. Whenever there is the opportunity, do not fail to be in the presence of such people. Take inspiration to continue sadhana through satsang.

Satsang is the surest cure for the dire disease of loneliness. Even in the midst of thousands of people, there are those who feel lonely. To relieve loneliness, a person may play badminton, mix in society and do similar things, but this is not the ultimate remedy; it is self-deception. In order to remove loneliness, sit alone and think of God. Make Him one's best friend and talk to Him mentally. This is also a form of satsang.

Living in that atmosphere which satsang creates will help the aspirant to always feel in tune with Him. People worship God as something apart from themselves, but forget that everyone is connected to God. Swami Sivananda once told me that he wanted me to visit different saints. I said, "I do not have to go at all because you have taught me everything." He said, "No, saints and yogis and great teachers are inspirers. Through satsang your devotion to God becomes strong. You may not get initiation from them, you don't even need to have a personal or private lesson from them, but you must seek their good wishes and blessings." So he sent me to Ramana Maharshi, Anandamayi Ma, Aurobindo and many others.

Swadhyaya

Self-study through reading spiritual books is *swadhyaya*. It is an essential part of yogic sadhana because it gives inspiration and at the same time encouragement and self-understanding from a spiritual perspective. When I was a student, I frequently read a marvellous book called *Imitation of Christ* by Thomas a' Kempis. Every time I read it, I had some new light. In the same manner, Swami Sivananda has also written some wonderful books which can help one to develop discrimination and to restructure one's whole nature. Without swadhyaya this cannot be done.

Sometimes an aspirant tires of sadhana. It is the nature of the mind to want a change. Reading spiritual books gives inspiration. There comes a stage in spiritual life when all the books have to be given up. That is a higher spiritual stage, where shastras and scriptures hold no truth, when experience can tell one more than books. That is an important stage and the aspirant must know where that stage begins. Otherwise the scriptures should be studied as a part of spiritual practice. This is known as swadhyaya. In the Yoga *Sutras* of Sage Patanjali it is written that tapasya, swadhyaya and ishwara pranidhana, faith in God are the three corollaries of sadhana.

The attitude of a sadhaka should be to read spiritual books for inspiration and to help recharge his battery. The attitude of a scholar is to go through the books and try to understand and compare them with other texts. It is said that whenever the scriptures are studied, it must be understood that is in order to find the highest truth, not in order to know something.

When the spiritual convictions and inspiration are in jeopardy, use swadhyaya as a means of reviving faith and re-establishing equanimity. Faith is reaffirmed by reading about the lives of great men and women who have attained self-realization despite suffering trials and tribulations. Swadhyaya is a practice which should be followed by the aspirant throughout life. It may not always be possible to avail oneself of the discourses of wise men and women, but spiritual texts can be studied at all times and in all places.

Satsang and swadhyaya, scriptural and self-study, are useful aids in spiritual life, but ultimately all that knowledge will have to be converted into personal experience and put it into practice. Without that, one can never aim at self-transformation. Listening to long discourses on meditation every day for many years will not give personal experience of meditation. In order to have that experience, one will have to develop

94

the practices and do them consistently each day without fail. Only then will one be able to witness any results.

Exhausting karma – tapasya and titiksha

During the practice of sadhana, it is inevitable that the sadhaka must undergo the consequences of both good and bad actions; that is the law of karma. Karma is not only what one has created in one's previous life; it is the total inheritance from previous generations and from the environment. In scientific terms it is called the molecular inheritance, the DNA molecules. This karma influences not only the course of one's destiny in general; it controls every movement, every action, every pain in the body, every thought that comes into the mind. The movement and behaviour of karmas is absolutely beyond man's comprehension. In order to exhaust a lot of karma, two methods have been suggested in the path of sadhana: tapasya and titiksha.

Tapasya means 'to burn, to heat'. It is purifying every part of the body through a particular process. To purify gold it is put in a fire; it is put through the process of tapasya. To purify one's karma, one exposes oneself to certain situations, for instance, living with a critical person rather than throwing him out because he is cleaning one's soul without water or soap. Tapasya is undergoing a process of suffering spontaneously and willingly. If this process of suffering is not undergone willingly, then nature will compel one to undergo it. If one is constipated, there will be either diarrhoea or piles or some other disease. If one willingly accepts doing the practice of shankhaprakshalana, it will be an arduous job for an hour or two, but it will relieve one of all the consequences of the karma of constipation. Otherwise there may be suffering for months or years instead of one and a half hours. So tapasya is a way to reduce the period of suffering which is due on account of one's karmas.

In the *Bhagavad Gita* different forms of tapasya, physical, mental and emotional austerity are given. Do not utter words which bring agitation into other people's minds. This austerity

95

pertains to speech. Different types of tapasya are intended to purify the habits, nature and content of the body and mind, so that the soul becomes free from the pressures of karma. Otherwise one has to undergo one's destiny; there is no other way.

Titiksha means endurance, being able to bear heat and cold, success and failure, praise and blame, and still remain in a balanced state of mind. In pleasure and pain, in gain and loss, in victory and defeat, the mind remains the same. Once the mind has been balanced, the sadhaka must be prepared to fight on the battlefield of life. Titiksha is resisting and tolerating when the mind is thrown into the extremes of life. When the body is exposed to extreme climates, when the mind is exposed to extreme situations, one should be able to balance it somehow. This is titiksha, the second method of exhausting the karma.

Develop willpower

Practising sadhana requires strong willpower. In order to strengthen the willpower, a small vow or decision has to be made at the very beginning of sadhana, at primary class level. Celibacy is a big vow, sitting in the middle of five fires is a big vow, sannyasa is a big vow. A simple, small vow can be made such as getting up early every morning, bathing and chanting Gayatri mantra, for instance, a specific number of times. Irrespective of workload, even if the health is suffering or if one has a cough and cold and is unable to do anything else, still one must get up and do it daily. In the same way, a vow can be made to fast on Ekadashi. Whatever vow is suitable for one's sadhana, it must then be followed with regularity. If the mind is disturbed, still it must be done. If faith in the vow dwindles, even then it must be done. The important point is that one has taken a vow, it must definitely be done.

The vow that is made is a form of will; it is a strong decision, a small oath. The principle of crystallization shows that if a small crystal is left hanging, after some time small crystal particles kept nearby are drawn to it, until in the end such a large crystal is formed. In this way the willpower becomes strong and the mind becomes disciplined. When the mind is strong, bad habits will change without recurring. Repentance has no effect because the mind is weak.

The symptoms of mental weakness are thinking too much and developing high blood pressure. Tension leads to loss of temper and anger. Such a weak mind will not be able to sustain the practice of sadhana. A weak mind is unable to do what it wants to do. One has positive ideas, but is unable to implement them. One knows what is right and wrong, but the tendency is not to follow it. Responsibilities are neglected; one knows one is irresponsible, but is unable to become stable. Because the mind is weak, one is attached to wrong actions and is unable to turn the mind away from them.

To make the body strong, go for walks, eat properly, exercise, participate in sports, practise yoga sadhana. To make the mind strong, one must be able to make a decision and stick to it without wavering.

Transcend intellect

For success in any spiritual sadhana, avoid intellectual analysis or explanation. Sadhana should only be done for practical reasons, devoid of all intellect, as intellectual analysis is supposed to be the greatest barrier. It does not bring spiritual progress as this type of scrutiny will bring the sadhana down from the intuitive level to the intellectual level.

Only when the mind and the intellect are transcended will the aspirant perceive the intuitive faculty, which is very powerful and a source of the most accurate knowledge. This is a pure experience which can be termed 'mindlessness', where the thought and the thinker merge into one another. No thoughts assail the aspirant at that point. That is the experience of the divine. How can this state be achieved? The sages have declared that it is primarily through personal effort and endeavour that anything is achieved in spiritual life. In the final analysis, it is only determined zeal and ceaseless effort that take one to the point of fulfilment.

One does not have to be intellectual to practise sadhana or even to understand it. Sadhana has to be practised to get the benefit. It is not necessary to know about it intellectually or even rationally. When those who are innocent and know very little about the practices take up sadhana, they progress very rapidly. Whatever sadhana is done to elevate the personality, it is better if nothing is studied about it. The spiritual teachings are very simple. No matter what the guru has said, no matter how high, low or deep he is, a sincere seeker can benefit from it. The benefit comes from within, not from outside; it has to be found inside. The guru only says, "The fountain is within you." It is up to the aspirant to go deep within. Intellect is a helper to some extent, but it becomes a barrier after a certain time, and has to be transcended.

No amount of scriptural study and reading will give realization. No amount of bookish and verbal knowledge will reveal the highest truth. It will destroy the tempo of sadhana. It may even subdue faith. In the course of time as sadhana progresses and deepens, scriptural knowledge will be revealed from within and one will be able to understand and discuss even without consulting any scripture or intellectual efforts. Wait patiently until intuition is awakened from within.

Do not think, but do sadhana spontaneously. Whatever sadhana has been learned, do it like a child, do not use the mind. The foundation of feeling is *shraddha*, faith, and the basis of intellect is argument. Intellect goes with argument; feeling and emotion with faith. There is no questioning. Where the intellect is concerned, there are always questions and answers. Sadhana is a subject of the heart, a subject of feeling and emotion, not of the mind or intellect.

The sadhaka who has been properly initiated and instructed in the science of sadhana and yoga should be careful not to compile various ideas which come from different sources of philosophy and usher in intellectual chaos. He should have nothing to do with various scriptures, beliefs, orders and congregations. If he consults these and forms his mental structure in accordance with the concepts contained in them, he will find it really hard to achieve the great spiritual power within.

Keep the mind free

Mental equilibrium is a preliminary process to sadhana. Divine grace descends upon those who have perfected mental poise. Take care of the mind and health. The mind and body sustain the soul. Constant work and mental engagement keep the inner instruments in order. Argument and reflection weakens the mind and is detrimental to normal progress in life. When the mind becomes quiet and peaceful, when there are fewer conflicts in the mind, one can clearly see into the affairs of life. The problem comes when one tries to settle matters through the intellect. The intellect is a confusing reality. Confusion cannot be cleared up with this confused intellect.

First attain peace of mind, one-pointedness and balance within, then try to settle matters. Shanti! Calm! Poise! Unruffled quiet! Enter inside. Repeat His name. Everlasting ananda is far beyond the mind and intellect.

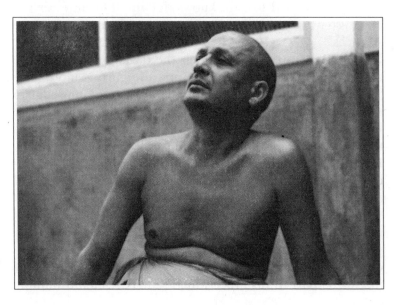

9

The Essence of Sadhana

GURU

In the *Shiva Samhita* (3:11) it is stated, "Only the knowledge imparted by a guru, through his lips, is powerful and useful, otherwise it becomes fruitless, weak and very painful." In fact, all the ancient texts state that for spiritual sadhana, especially the higher esoteric practices, the guru is indispensable. From all points of view this is a logical claim. The guidance of a teacher is needed to gain knowledge in all faculties or sciences, so why doubt the necessity of a guide for the spiritual sciences.

Guru means one who dispels the darkness of ignorance and brings illumination. Therefore, the guru is more than just a teacher. A teacher can only give academic knowledge to satisfy and stimulate the intellect, but the guru gives intuitive knowledge through intimate experience. He has realized his true self by dint of his own sadhana and rigorous disciplines. He has travelled the same path which the aspirants are stumbling along and knows the pitfalls and dangers that may befall the disciple.

The path is hazardous, narrow as a razor's edge and few who have traversed it know the way. A sadhaka is not even sure of the destination, so how can he assume to know the way? However, the guru has been there and his return to show the way is part of his grace which sadhakas should humbly acknowledge. The divine powers have unfolded in him and revealed the unknown mysteries of spirit. Not only has he discovered the hidden reality for himself, but he can also transmit the experience to others to encourage them on the same path. In fact, such a guru lives for just this purpose: to awaken the yearning for spiritual knowledge in others.

Spiritual evolution

The basis of all spiritual sadhana is personal evolution. Culturally, socially, racially and politically all may be the same, but in terms of spiritual evolution no two persons are at the same point. Who can know at which rung of the ladder one is poised? Spiritual sadhana has to begin from the point one is at. It is the guru alone who can judge this, by examining the karma and personal evolution of an aspirant, and giving a sadhana on that basis. This insight is very important, as progress depends upon the suitability and efficacy of the practised sadhana. Moreover, the path of spiritual sadhana is through the deepest layers of the mind, where all the skeletons of past experiences are residing. An encounter with them can be dangerous for one's equilibrium, if it is not done under the watchful guidance of a guru.

Sometimes the aspirant may have already evolved through sadhana done in previous lives, but in order to pick up the loose threads he requires the hand of a master craftsman. In spiritual life, the power with which the aspirant is playing is the same power that has created him, that of consciousness. It is a delicate matter, requiring the skill of a professional. The guru has this skill. Spiritual sadhana can never be chosen on the personal whim of the sadhaka. It is the guru alone who has the authority, insight and experience to judge which sadhana is best for an aspirant. However, the guru's interest in the disciple's sadhana is motivated only by the disciple's sincerity.

The guru initiates the aspirant into sadhana and gives the inspiration to remain on the path in spite of any difficulties that may assail him. Initiation is an important factor before beginning any sadhana. The guru's initiation is power-charged and creates a suitable atmosphere and mental equilibrium to fulfil the obligations of the spiritual practice and thereby receive the merits of sadhana. It is stated in the tantra shastras that without initiation from a guru, sadhana cannot induce the desired results.

To progress in sadhana, the disciple must adhere strictly to the guru's teachings. In the beginning, the sadhana given by the guru may seem too easy or even inconsequential, and the sadhaka may dismiss the whole thing, thinking that the guru is not really interested. The belief that the guru knows what is suitable in terms of sadhana must be firmly maintained, even though the practices may not seem suitable. For instance, the guru may tell the disciple that the sadhana consists of ten minutes asana, ten minutes pranayama, ten minutes japa and half an hour reading books on kundalini yoga. The disciple may wonder why the sadhana is not more difficult, especially as he is capable of much more. The disciple may be able to do wonderful asanas and continue for an hour or more, but that may be the first test to which the guru is subjecting the sadhaka.

Sadhana given by the guru helps to extract the ego and eliminate the karma of the disciple, if it is practised without expectation. Acceptance of the guru's guidance without anticipation of any merit implies subjugation of one's ego. Whatever one decides to do oneself involves the ego. However, when the guru instructs the aspirant, it is not one's own desire but the guru's order that motivates him. When there is no desire, there is no expectation, no delusion, and through this subtle process the disciple evolves.

AWARENESS

Awareness is the witnessing principle, the actionless aspect that is associated with consciousness, Shiva or Purusha. That awareness is present even now in every human being. Because of that awareness, one knows that one is doing something,

102

thinking something, and at the same time, one is aware of it, one is a witness of it. This awareness is not found in an animal, because at that stage of evolution the awareness is undeveloped; it is dormant, it is sleeping. Therefore, an animal does many things but it is not aware of its actions.

When this awareness which has developed in man from the beginning leaves the portals of the body and mind, it becomes completely pure. When body consciousness and mental consciousness are activated with this pure consciousness, that is known as cosmic consciousness. Cosmic awareness has no form. It is not in the form of attention or in the form of thought either. It is just a kind of awareness.

Pure awareness is the be-all and end-all of the sadhaka. It is never tired, never loses patience, never loses courage, never gets confused, but remains awake forever. That is the form of awareness required for ultimate success in sadhana, and usually it is not properly understood because there is no fundamental conception of the word 'awareness'. This awareness is existence and it remains even at night when one is deeply asleep. It is through sadhana that this awareness develops and expands.

Panorama of awareness within

During sadhana practices all the sense channels begin to withdraw and it is at that time that one becomes aware of troubles and anxieties. In the same way, obstructing the passages of experience that contribute to the activities of the brain is one of the methods of stimulating the consciousness, *samskaras* and *vasanas*, latent impressions and desires. It is like digging. In this practice the sense organs are being obstructed. One by one, all these channels should be obstructed, not in order to inhibit them, but to enable one to sit quietly and see the fantastic panorama of awareness inside, which at present is not available due to the extroverted tendency.

It is said in the *Bhagavad Gita* that consciousness is constantly fluctuating because that is its nature. In sadhana two factors bring about absolute steadiness. One is *abhyasa*, persistent practice, and the other is *vairagya*, complete detachment from the insignificant, irrelevant and meaningless affairs of life. Further, in the *Bhagavad Gita* it is said, "Even as a tortoise withdraws its limbs inside when they are not required, in the same way the yogi has to withdraw his senses from sense objects; then his awareness becomes steady, otherwise not." However, it must also be understood that in the earliest stages of sadhana, concentration, tense effort, working hard to focus the mind will not give any positive result. It may appear that the whole process of awareness is being hurried up, but ultimately the aspirant will realize that he will not be able to walk further.

Each *indriya* or sense organ is a channel which contributes to the influence on the brain, and if one of the channels is obstructed, then the mental experience becomes very keen. Usually when people do their work, they are not at all aware of their mental problems and distractions, although they are there. However, when all the work is finished and they sit down for sadhana, all the thoughts start coming. It is not because thoughts only happen at that time; the thoughts were also there at other times, but then the sense channels were not obstructed. Everything was functioning externally, and there

104

was no awareness of what was going on inside. The *vritti*, the mental attitude, was extroverted.

The mind functions under two attitudes: *bahiranga mukha vritti*, external awareness, and *antaranga mukha vritti*, internal awareness. External awareness has its basis in the sense organs and through this attitude the mind becomes extrovert. In *Kathopanishad* it says, "Man does not see the higher self because his consciousness is drawn to external objects by the senses and, in fact, the senses are the root cause of this extroverted tendency of the mind." If one lights a candle and at the same time keeps the fan running, the flame can never become steady. In the same way, it is written in the *Bhagavad Gita*, "Just as a lamp can remain absolutely steady in a place without any breeze or wind, so the practitioner of yoga should try to avoid the cause of that wind or breeze which brings about mental fluctuations." Awareness must be developed in the proper manner, so that one is able to become the impartial observer of these states of mind.

Developing awareness
During sadhana, when one is able to withdraw the mind from external experiences and inner awareness blooms in some form or other, that is the inner path. When a person looks towards the outside world, the world of the senses and the mind, then the external objects of cognition, the gross manifestation of divinity, of creation, is experienced. This happens all the time, but when one tries to cognize a thought, a feeling, an emotion or passion, it cannot be done. Its impact can be felt, but it cannot be cognized. That is the first limitation in sadhana. The aspirant should go through this in the course of sadhana, and then, in the same manner, the patterns of the mind should be seen.

Yantras and mandalas are forms of higher realities. Paintings by talented artists, including abstract art, are like the forms of feeling, emotion, fear, jealousy, love, compassion, that one should be able to see within. Such is the doorway to subtle awareness, which leads to the inner path of sadhana.

105

When mental and emotional feelings can be perceived in concrete form, just like seeing a picture outside, then one has withdrawn from external to internal. This is the meaning of internal awareness. Until then, a person is gross, just external, roving over the instinctive plane of animals, and not beyond that. This is a symptom or indication. When a ghost is seen in a graveyard, it is one's absolute and total fear personified. That is its form. In the same way, love and compassion also have forms.

At first, the object of one's concentration shines only for a short while. Later, one begins to retain it, and finally it becomes stabilized and remains. The form will shine and illumine itself in the dark areas of one's consciousness. That is the path of spiritual sadhana. It makes no difference whether the object of concentration is guru, ishta or a particular symbol. The path is only one. One person may concentrate on the shivalingam, another may concentrate on Krishna, a cross or a flame of fire; it is all the same. The paths are not different. The goal is one and the paths of sadhana are one.

Therefore, the aspirant should try to withdraw and awaken the consciousness simultaneously, not one after the other, not one before the other. If awakening takes place before withdrawal, one will be schizophrenic and if withdrawal takes place without awakening, it will be hypnosis. A person will be in meditation for three hours without any experience and come out with nothing, because there was only withdrawal from the external world of perception, from the world of the senses.

Withdrawal is not final. One has to withdraw, but simultaneously one has to awaken that tiny flame of consciousness which one has chosen to meditate upon, such as the form of a candle flame. That tiny flame is the replica of one's consciousness. Whether a blue lotus, red lotus, shivalingam, cross or symbol of Om, they are all replicas or symbols of consciousness, and this replica of consciousness must be maintained with unbroken awareness. Unbroken awakening of consciousness and systematic withdrawal of external awareness is the link which leads to spiritual awakening in sadhana.

Subtle awareness

When aspirants begin to become established in sadhana, a subtle awareness develops which enables them to look within. With this awareness they are able to transcend the external mind, external experiences, and the very stuff of their existence called the ego. Then they begin to realize that this body, this name, this nationality, this empirical definition is not the ultimate explanation, but merely definitions of this external appearance.

If the aspirant progresses in sadhana and is able to go beyond the body, then comes the mind and its vrittis. Is the

107

mind the definition of ultimate awareness? Is happiness, un-happiness, love, hatred, agony, joy, past, present and future the definition? Do these experiences being undergone in this life belong to me? These diverse, conflicting experiences which break the body, personality and mind, throughout life, do not belong to me. 'I am not this'.

Beyond body and mind

If one goes on analyzing and trying to understand, it will be found that all that one has been thinking and experiencing about oneself does not exist. When in sadhana, in meditation, one goes deep within one's own self, within the dimensions of total equanimity and samadhi, then the sadhaka is a different person altogether. The experience of that 'I' and the experience of the present 'I' are different. The experience of this present 'I' is covered with notions of duality and multiplicity. There is no awareness of unity. As long as there is the experience of the present 'I', unity cannot be experienced. Only duality can be experienced, and therefore conflict. Multiplicity and diversity do not bring unity. Unless unity is experienced, the higher self cannot be experienced.

This experience of *aham*, the cosmic 'I', emerges in sadhana when one goes deeper and deeper, not into one's own body, mind or personality, but into one's own self. This self is not confined to this body just as energy is not confined to one particular point. Energy is universal. Spirit, *atma*, the cosmic self, are universal. By mistake, one identifies that self with this body because one knows this body as oneself; but the spirit, the atma, the cosmic self, is not confined to this body. It is not in the body, it is beyond the body. The body is in the self because the body is limited and the cosmic self, the atma, is not limited.

The cosmic self is the finest experience of human life and that experience is called *atma jnana*. *Atma* means the cosmic self, the infinite self, the real self, the total self, not the little self, the egotistical self, the physical or mental self. *Jnana* means awareness, knowledge and experience. This is the ul-

108

timate awareness in sadhana. As far as sadhana is concerned, if one can be aware of God just as one is constantly aware of the pain in a wound, it is called *surati*, constant awareness of God. If this awareness comes, one is lucky and blessed.

Awareness of the spiritual dimension is the first step in the march by the divine to victory over the animal in man, and certainly it is not possible to practise sadhana with steadfast attention immediately. It may take years of effort. In fact, perfection of sadhana takes twelve years. However, emphasis is to be placed on awareness and sadhakas are encouraged to explore and learn about the various aspects of their personality through yoga sadhana. Positive transformation is a natural process which occurs as a result of regular sadhana performed with full awareness, not through forcing the mind and body to the limit and beyond. Self-realization is the goal. Awareness of the goal will maintain the spirit for sadhana.

The scriptures state only the bare essentials as guidelines for sadhakas. Secrets for success in sadhana can only be learned under the guidance of a guru, and are only revealed to the most deserving aspirants. In this manner the purity of yoga sadhana is preserved for humanity.

INNER SILENCE

The practice of inner silence, inner peace, is essential for success in spiritual sadhana. It is regarded as a secret element of sadhana, and at the appropriate time in sadhana, according to the guru-disciple tradition, the sadhaka is initiated into the proper techniques. Inner silence is the true definition of silence, for silence is not the silence of speech. In inner silence, thought vibrations are stopped and finally remain suspended. The true meaning of inner silence will be understood if the thoughts that enter the mind are regarded as forms of mental disturbance. These mental disturbances prevent the experience of self-realization.

Inner silence is not 'not thinking'; it is really a positive state, when the sadhaka is either remembering the name or the form instead of all and sundry. Inner peace is dynamic. Sleep and lethargy do not represent inner peace. Thoughts should not come to the mind, except for the name and the feelings of His presence and divinity. This will bestow mental strength as well as psychological diversion. Once inner peace is obtained, nothing can shake the soul. Once established in this peace, sadhana becomes powerful and leads to self-realization.

Even though the complete course of inner silence is lengthy, one technique must be adopted to create a state of thoughtlessness. 'Stop thinking' is the 'Open Sesame' of sadhana, so learn the real art of sitting quietly. Give up the habit of merely sitting or lying quietly, and do not daydream, as it will undo one's achievements. However, it is very difficult to sit quietly because the inner mind is always active, except when one truly meditates.

The less one thinks, the greater one becomes. Thoughts of various kinds kill spiritual stamina. Control the thoughts by means of sadhana; learn the art of pratyahara, concentration, and karma yoga. Keep the mind calm, quiet and serene for just a few minutes every day and try to practise inner silence all day on Sundays. There is no end to friendly invitations. Don't waste a single moment; the destination is still far. Close the eyes and become aware of silence, even if for a moment. Practise this mental silence in the form of swadhyaya; in the practice of antar mouna; sing His names, and do japa. These are all positive methods of initiating mental peace. One can practise outside in the open or inside a room where there will be less disturbance.

Antar mouna

The principal method of *antar mouna* or inner silence has five stages. First, see as a witness all the thoughts which come and go, appear and disappear in the mind. In the second stage, pose any one thought at will and remove it and then enter a state of vacuum. The third stage is to rotate the mind around any one subject by thinking everything about it. In the fourth

110

stage, be alert and careful and create a state of vacuum. In the final stage, one has to be completely detached, as an impartial witness. Practise this in a place where the atmosphere is restful, happy, contented and joyful. It can and should also be practised in the midst of noise and crowds. It is more easily practised after pranayama or if one is exhausted, because then the mind is often quieter and one is able to gain at least a little distance from its endless activities.

Inner silence or the state of thoughtlessness gradually envelops the three worlds: the external or gross, the internal or subtle, and the causal. When it envelops the causal region, all worldly desires are dissolved and the sense of duality ceases and one's sadhana will then be able to move into another dimension of consciousness.

REGULARITY

There is a great law in the life of a spiritual aspirant regarding spiritual practice. It is not the quantum of practice, not just a question of finding a suitable sadhana, but the regularity one maintains in its performance that is important. As long as one is regular in one's yoga practices, even if one can only devote a minimum period of time, one will definitely travel very far into one's inner self. Sadhana should be practised regularly just like washing the face and brushing the teeth in the morning. Even if not much can be done, practise one thing daily, at a fixed time, either in the morning or at night. Some people do pooja daily, some swadhyaya, others do asana, pranayama, japa or chanting of *Ramayana*. Choose one sadhana and do it daily.

Even if people want to devote their whole life to yoga and spiritual achievements, they are not able to do so. They cannot even spare ten minutes for asanas and pranayama. Therefore, people with spiritual aspirations should start with the minimum amount of time. Instead of trying to devote two or three hours every day, which will gradually reduce to nil anyway, it is preferable to first start with ten minutes.

111

One sadhana will have to be decided on, one practice to be done at any cost, with absolute regularity, according to temperament and inclination. If ten minutes has been decided on, then practise only for ten minutes. One may not be well mentally, there may be a lot of preoccupations, no interest in the practice at all, or even lack of faith in it, but still it must be done at any cost. That sadhana will have to be done because a resolve has been made. Make those ten minutes a regular practice, so that in the course of time  all the energies and interests are crystallized, and one will definitely be able to travel very far in one's inner self. The time of practice will then automatically increase according to necessity, capacity and motivation.

When I received a mantra from my guru, he told me one thing, "Practise five malas every day, without fail!" Even now I practise it. There was a time, even after initiation, when I changed my philosophy completely and became an atheist. I did not believe in God, but I continued my mantra practice, not because I believed in it, but because I had to do it regularly. To establish regularity takes time, not just six months. It can easily take two or three years, after which one can say, "Yes, regularity has been established." But even then one must be regular, which means daily practice of sadhana.

Do not think which practice is more important or which is superior or more effective. Only think which practice can be stuck to and carried through. Whether kriya yoga is more powerful or asanas are more effective is not the consideration. The important thing is whether one will be able to continue with the practice at any cost. When a suitable sadhana has been selected, it must be practised every day, and at the same time the aspirant must become a participant in the daily scheme of life.

Maintaining continuity in sadhana

To start practising sadhana is not difficult, but to continue is difficult. Irregularity in sadhana is the first main obstacle that has to be crossed. Some means must be found to remove it, otherwise one will not get anywhere. External causes do not obstruct the sadhana; laziness and indifference constitute the chief obstacles to regularity. If time cannot be found during the day, one should do japa mentally and remember God's name anywhere, anytime.

Whether the practice is asana, pranayama, hatha yoga, raja yoga, bhakti yoga or something else, it is very difficult to maintain regularity in spiritual practice for at least a few years. In real sadhana even a day's break disturbs the entire old order completely and one cannot restart at the same point. That is one of the most peculiar things on the path of spiritual experience. Knowledge can be restarted from the point where one left off, but sadhana must be restarted from the beginning. That is a difficult point in sadhana.

In the spiritual quest, one is not trying to accumulate knowledge but a personal experience of that knowledge, and this experience can only be obtained by constant and consist-ent effort in one's practices. If sadhana is practised for a year and then left for six months, the aspirant can no longer say that he has practised for a year. That period of sadhana is lost as far as experience is concerned. However, in intellectual knowledge nothing has been lost. The path of knowledge can be resumed from the point where it was left, but experience must be started again from the beginning. Therefore, because the ultimate aim of the spiritual quest is not just knowledge but personal experience, one must be regular. It is not the time spent, but the continuity that is important. This constancy of practice is called *abhyasa*. In that lies the secret of success.

In conclusion, regular sadhana constitutes the basis for the descent of higher consciousness. This point needs to be understood by every spiritual aspirant, whether a beginner or someone practising higher sadhana. All those who are sincere must endeavour to keep the time for sadhana fixed and steady. Be aware that the path of spiritual practice and the attainment of perfection is difficult in the early stages; in the middle it becomes active and energizing, and finally it becomes successful. All those whose determination is steady and whose faith is resolute will attain without effort that plane where their ishta is present. This is savikalpa samadhi.

Start from where one is

The scheme of sadhana cannot be the same for everybody. Qualitatively, by religion and nationality people may be the same, but spiritually, from the point of view of evolution of consciousness, no two people are the same. Every sadhaka has his own karma, his own personality, his own desires, passions, idiosyncrasies and infirmities.

Not every aspirant is strong enough to bear the brunt of penance and austere sadhana. Many times one may want to have a high experience, but at the same time the fabric of one's existence is so flimsy and weak that one succumbs to the ordinary desires of life, unable to live without sense gratification, attachments and addictions. What happens to this sadhaka? Can he realize his own self or not? Can he experience the highest consciousness with all the idiosyncrasies of his life, or is it necessary for him to become a puritan?

If sadhana is practised with sincerity, in time it will be found that the external self has been transcended. In the scheme of evolution, each individual is standing at a particular point. Start from there. Do not try to jump onto another's platform and start the journey from there. It will be a mistake. That self, that atma, which will be experienced through sadhana is beyond all these external definitions. These external limitations and references do not taint this effulgent, spiritual consciousness, which one is.

114

10

Components of Sadhana

GRACE

The path of mundane life ends with reasoning, with intellectualizing. When reason has failed and the intellect cannot produce supramental experiences any more, the last thing left is called *prasad*, the grace that comes from the guru, the grace that comes from within one's own self. Guru's grace is most difficult to comprehend, and even more difficult to explain. In India, the phrase commonly used to emphasize the importance of guru's grace in the aspirants' life is: *Guru kripa hi kevalam*, which means that guru's grace alone can liberate a disciple.

Grace or *anugraha* is also known as *shaktipat*. The intensity of shaktipat depends on the intensity of a disciple's desire to attain realization, and his previous samskaras. Spiritually evolved souls can attain enlightenment through intense, *tivra*, shaktipat without performing much sadhana. Those who are less evolved receive *madhyama* shaktipat to help them realize their guru and to be initiated into sadhana. Through patience and regular practice of sadhana they can attain liberation. The third type of shaktipat is moderate, *manda*, which instils a yearning for spiritual knowledge. If the desire is pursued with perseverance in the quest, there can be enlightenment.

Grace has to be earned by spiritual discipline and desire. It cannot be bought, nor can the guru be cheated. There are four main ways, or *upayas*, described in the *Shiva Sutras* to purify the body and mind and earn this grace: anavopaya, shaktopaya, shambhavopaya and anupaya. *Anavopaya* is the most gross of the four upaya sadhanas of tantra. It includes physical discipline, such as hatha yoga sadhana, which purifies the body and awakens sushumna. It is also known as *kriyopaya*.

Shaktopaya is a means of approaching the divine reality through shakti. It is for a person whose mind and body are already considerably pure. It consists of concentration, mantra repetition and instilling the idea that 'I am the supreme consciousness. The universe is none other than expansion of the Self'. This sadhana is also known as *jnanopaya* because it utilizes the aspect of jnana. Kundalini rises by means of the higher intellect and therefore it includes jnana yoga sadhana and other higher stages of raja yoga sadhana.

Shambhavopaya is for those who are highly evolved, who can become realized by simply concentrating on the idea of pure consciousness or the shiva tattwa. Through a sadhana of constant self-analysis, awareness and reflection, they are led to self realization. This is the path of adwaita philosophy.

Anupaya is direct realization through one simple action of the guru. *Anu* denotes something minute, the nucleus of the nucleus. Thus anupaya means the grace which is attained by nominal or no effort. It is only possible for very advanced aspirants. A well-known example is when Balkrishna opened his mouth and his adopted mother, Yashoda, saw the entire universe. Anupaya is therefore also known as *anandopaya* because it instils instant bliss.

DIET AND SADHANA

Diet should be considered as a part of sadhana. When practising sadhana, food is not taken for sense gratification, but to sustain the vehicle of the indweller, the atma. Eating 'to please Shiva' means that when taking food, the yogi should not feel that he is eating for himself. He should cultivate the

attitude that he is nourishing the body for its maintenance so
his consciousness can continue its process of unfoldment and
spiritual evolution. Shiva is the inner consciousness, the atma.
Everything the yogi eats should be considered as prasad, an
offering from the supreme being. This is very important for
eradicating the sense of ego: 'I' want and 'I' eat. Therefore,
a sadhaka should take food as if it is an offering to God, not
merely as lunch or dinner. Food should be regarded as an
offering for a sacrifice.

   In some forms of sadhana there are no restrictions, unless
a person is suffering from a serious disease. However, veg-
etarianism is a must for those who want to practise pranayama
for higher concentration. Therefore, there are disciplines according to the need of the aspirant. There are various stages
of sadhana. When one starts practising sadhana, it does not
matter what one eats or how one lives. However, if after some
time the aspirant decides to delve more deeply into the spiritual path, he will have to choose which way he wants to go.
Either the path of tantric evolution or the path of raja yoga
evolution can be followed. If proceeding along the tantric

117

path, then a non-vegetarian diet may be used as a tool, if it is part of the spiritual ritual. If proceeding along the path of hatha yoga, bhakti yoga or jnana yoga, it is recommended that the aspirant becomes a total vegetarian.

If one is following the path of raja yoga and it is necessary to sit for two or three hours of japa or meditation, then a light vegetarian diet is preferable. During long periods of meditation, the inner body temperature, which is responsible for digestion, comes down. A non-vegetarian diet requires a higher body temperature for proper functioning of the digestive process. If the raja yoga practitioner eats heavy food and then practises sadhana, eventually dyspepsia, high blood pressure, rheumatism and coronary problems will result.

With the practice of meditation or mantra yoga, not only does the inner body temperature drop, but the digestive secretions and enzymes are also reduced. For proper digestion, five digestive secretions are required in the correct proportions along with the correct body temperature, which varies in different areas of the body. In the small intestine a constant temperature is required for a long period of time. In the stomach a higher temperature is needed for about three or four hours only, otherwise hyperacidity and ulcers may develop. If the temperature is lower, there will be hypoacidity or indigestion. Similarly, if the temperature in the small intestine is higher, diarrhoea, dysentery or colitis will result. If it is lower, gastric problems and poor assimilation will result.

These temperatures are affected by prolonged, intensive periods of meditation, so if this is part of the daily sadhana, the diet will have to be adjusted or the diet greatly reduced. Firstly, vegetables should be well boiled so that the low temperature of the body does not disturb the digestion. Secondly, some digestive enzymes and acids should be added to the food to aid the digestive function. Certain foods such as papaya, pineapple and bean sprouts contain digestive enzymes. Spices such as coriander, pepper, turmeric, aniseed, cumin, cayenne, mustard and garlic are all digestives, as are herbs such as mint, alfalfa, tulsi or basil and chamomile.

118

A yogi should always regard food as a medicine which will purify and fuel the body and mind for the maintenance of life and progress in sadhana. Thus at all times he will eat cautiously, with awareness and with a higher purpose rather than for sensual pleasure.

Moderation in eating

The general rule is to eat what is necessary to maintain the requirements of the body and to choose a diet which will be most conducive to one's sadhana. *Mitahara*, moderation in diet, means eating sparingly, neither overeating nor under-eating. For maximum digestive functioning it is said that the stomach should be filled fifty percent with solids, twenty-five with liquids and the remaining twenty-five percent with air or empty. Thus, the body and mind remain healthy and balanced. A weak body cannot support a strong mind. A strong, healthy body reflects the nature of the mind. Overeating and greediness for food shows an uncontrolled mind. The diet should be simple and pure, and the food light, sattwic, digestible and well-cooked, according to the season. As Swami Sivananda points out, "Heavy food leads to a tamasic state and induces sleep. There is a general misapprehension that a large quantity of food is necessary for health and strength. Much depends upon the power of assimilation and absorption. Generally, in the vast majority of cases, most of the food passes away undigested along with faeces. Almost all diseases are due to eating irregularly, overeating and unwholesome food."

The time of eating is also important because digestion follows the solar rhythm very closely. Hence the peak digestive period is between eleven am and one pm. Taking the main meal at this time will help to avoid many digestive problems. Also, taking a light breakfast when the sun is rising, and a light dinner when the sun is setting means the digestive process is completed early and one is able to do one's sadhana and sleep with a light stomach and a free mind. Regularity in meals and meal timings helps to maintain a high energy level necessary

119

for progress in sadhana. Try to follow the middle path in regard to diet, neither too much nor too little. Excess food increases tamas, heaviness and dullness, while insufficient food causes weakness and an inability to concentrate.

Fasting

Swami Sivananda says, "Occasional fasting once a month or when passion troubles the sadhaka will suffice." Though fasting has a lot to offer and many people advocate it, a person who devotes many hours to hatha yoga sadhana should not strain the body in such a way. Proper care of the body should

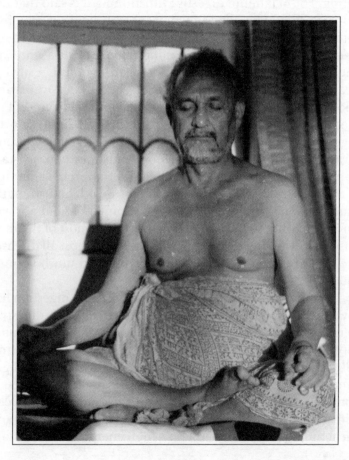

be taken and any unnecessary strain or injury avoided, as the body is the vehicle to higher consciousness. Of course, the aspirant has to be sensible about these instructions and take into account the situation and conditions.

In India many people follow the age-old tradition of fasting in conjunction with the phases of the moon. Particular days are conducive to either a full or half-day fast, for example, the fourth, ninth, eleventh, fourteenth and fifteenth days of either the bright or dark fortnight. However, diet differs according to each individual, so the aspirant may have to experiment with different foods and quantities before finding the correct diet for his sadhana, to help purify the body and stabilize the mind and passions. Do not become too food conscious and indulge in fads. Consciousness lies beyond diet. The body and mind are definitely influenced by diet, but there is something more, which is consciousness. Consciousness is beyond the body and mind, and diet has no influence on its evolution. Whether one eats fruit, raw or cooked vegetables, cheese, butter, beef or ham makes no difference to consciousness. However, a pure and moderate diet helps establish equilibrium and creates conditions conducive to higher experiences.

THE BEST TIME FOR SADHANA

Why is it necessary to get up early in the morning to practise sadhana? It is related to the energy crisis, the lack of internal energy that many people feel. The brain has many energy patterns which are cyclic and work like a clock. At one time a certain cycle may be at its maximum point while another cycle may be near its minimum. The energy is at different levels during the twenty-four period, as well as varying with the seasons and with many other factors known and unknown.

The day has a particular energy cycle in which the pranic rhythms gradually increase from four am and reach their peak at midday. The prana is static from midday to four pm and then starts to diminish. After sunset it falls very rapidly

121

and between midnight and four am it is minimal. Not acting according to this cycle leads to tiredness and an inability to fulfil one's daily commitments. The best time for sadhana is from four to six in the morning when both the solar or vital system and the lunar or mental system are active. As a result sushumna nadi flows freely and therefore meditation becomes easier. These two systems start working together between four and six am. During this time, when both the mental and pranic systems are functioning, meditation is spontaneous, without any difficulty. That is the purpose of practising sadhana in this period, known as *brahmamuhurta*.

Scientists are now aware of the internal body cycles and the importance of maintaining them for health and clarity of mind. Chemicals in the brain are responsible not only for the physical state, but also for the mental state and one's perception of the environment and of who one is, at any given moment. Yogis are also aware of the importance of keeping the internal environment clean and pure, and of manipulating it so as to produce an atmosphere conducive to higher experiences. They have developed methods of regulating the brain chemicals naturally so as to optimize the ability to tap human potential. Getting up early in the morning is a part of their sadhana and lifestyle. It is a means to manipulate the internal body secretions so that one can flow more smoothly from day to day as well as being more open to spiritual experience.

The energy level is lowest between two and four in the morning. Proper rest is essential for sadhakas, not getting up at two am, which is the time when heart attacks and birth deliveries are most commonly reported. Between four and six am there are certain secretions in the physical body which are necessary for concentration and meditation. Practising sadhana during this period will increase energy levels. One will be less prone to heart attacks, because meditation is an antidote to stress and helps to reverse the processes which are thought to lead to heart attacks. Sleeping during this period means the physical body will run all day at a low energy level.

Therefore, the best time to practise sadhana is the period between four and six am, brahmamuhurta. Brahmamuhurta is not necessarily related to the rising of the sun. At the North Pole, where people do not see the sun for days, they still have a time for sleeping and waking. They practise their sadhana on waking, which is brahmamuhurta for them. Brahmamuhurta is the time of day which is most auspicious for the practice of any spiritual sadhana. At this time only sadhakas are up and everyone else is sleeping.

Place and atmosphere

Sadhana practised at the same time every day and in the same appointed place is infinitely more fruitful than practising at varying hours and in different places. When sadhana is practised in a particular place over an extended period, that place absorbs the positive vibrations emanating from within and the atmosphere becomes charged. When sitting in that place, one will spontaneously drift into a state of tranquillity and oneness. In this way, the whole process becomes much easier. Anyone who enters the sadhana place will feel the effect of the positive vibrations that have been created.

The place of sadhana and the atmosphere has to be conducive to spiritual practice. The place must be quiet and free from disturbance which can distract the practitioner. It is best to find some corner or spot in one's home which is relatively or completely isolated. Keep the sadhana room like a temple, not like a bedroom or slumber room. It should contain only sacred objects like pictures of saints, guru, scriptures and so on. Keep a mat or a cushion for use during the period of sadhana and keep it for that purpose only. A mosquito net may also be required for meditation practice. Such things should be taken into account. At the appointed time, wash the hands and face and, if possible, light some incense or an oil lamp. Sit down in an asana or steady cross-legged posture for meditation or whatever the practice is. Set a fixed time and place for sadhana practice and strive to maintain it.

123

KEEPING THE TRADITION ALIVE

Any instructions related to sadhana in the literature are given only as guidelines. Many authors try to explain the practices as well as possible, but still it is necessary to learn the techniques from a guru who has had personal experience with the techniques. This is not only true for yoga sadhana but with most sciences.

Throughout history, the yogic tradition and many other sciences have been passed on from guru to disciple. However, in many cases these traditions have been interrupted due to political upheavals, migrations and destruction. Many scriptures have also been destroyed and so the scriptural tradition alone cannot be relied upon. Scriptural tradition means the sadhanas recorded in the tantric scriptures and Upanishads. The thirty minor Upanishads talk about the ultimate nature of reality, but at the same time they discuss different sadhanas for approaching reality, whereas the ten major Upanishads explain the nature of the ultimate being and our status in the cosmic reality, but no sadhana is given. Today we are able to translate the teachings contained in these scriptures into modern day language. Maybe after a hundred years or so, today's writings will again be recast in another fashion according to the nature of the people who exist then.

I talk about sadhana and I write about it in books which are read today and which will be rewritten after a few centuries. I teach yoga sadhana to my disciples and they teach others. In this manner the tradition will continue for centuries, not the practices, not the science as a whole, but just the idea of sadhana. This is the guru-student tradition, and it is how the spiritual tradition of sadhana has to be kept alive, keeping in mind that accidents can take place in history.

11

Sadhana and the Balance of Life

Many people who have done too much sadhana without taking care to balance and harmonize their inner and outer life have either had bad experiences or have become very ill. While all sincere sadhakas should have an aspiration to unlock their inner potential, at the same time they should try to make sure that the inner and outer life is balanced at all levels. Do not be in too much of a hurry to progress in sadhana. The process should be slow but sure, which will allow the body, mind and emotions to adjust to new and more refined levels of functioning.

The path of darkness and the path of light

In the Indian scriptures, the simultaneous awakening and balance of ida and pingala is called the path of light, the path of the *devas*, divine beings. This is the path of sadhana, where there is simultaneous expansion of inner awareness combined with corresponding action in the outside world. In the *Ishavasya Upanishad* (v. 9), it is said, "Those who follow the path of *avidya* (ignorance, action in the outside world) enter into blinding darkness. Conversely, those who are engrossed in *vidya* (inner knowledge of the mind, or more specifically meditation practices) also enter into still greater blinding darkness." This is a clear statement that should be remembered by both those who try to open up ida, the inner world, alone through sadhana and those who are concerned only with pingala, worldly activities – both will remain deluded.

The same idea is further expanded in the next verse: "The wise ones have told us that meditation practices alone and external activity alone will each give a different result." A certain level of understanding is attained by total concern with worldly activities; another level of understanding is attained by total concern with exploring the mind through esoteric practices. Eventually, however, each becomes a block to further progress. The text continues in verse 11: "He who knows both vidya (the inner world) and avidya (the outer world) crosses the abyss of death through avidya and attains immortality through vidya." These three verses are probably the most important ones in upanishadic literature and studying them gives great insight into the meaning of sadhana.

In regard to sadhana, both extroversion and introversion must be practised together. Neither must be rejected. One must simultaneously do meditation practices to unfold inner awareness and also work. There should be continual observation of and alertness to the inner process of the mind, while simultaneously acting in the world. This is the path of light, the path of the devas. Balance is given to both ida and pingala. One becomes a person of inner knowledge while acting in the world. Both karma yoga, the yoga of action, and dhyana yoga, the yoga of meditation, are combined and integrated into one's life.

The meaning of the word 'death' in verse 11 is not death in the usual sense. It means the death of delusion, the death of *laya*, loss of awareness, during meditation practices. Laya is the greatest block during sadhana; it is the obstacle of unconsciousness. People reach a certain stage in their practices where they are unable to maintain awareness. They get lost in a hazy reverie or fall asleep. To progress in unfolding the dormant potential and to tread the spiritual path, one must pass beyond this laya.

The method of overcoming this obstacle is by doing karma yoga and by interacting with the outside world. Laya indicates excessive tamas in one's nature. By intense karma yoga the nature can be elevated so that it becomes more rajasic, which will counteract the tendency for laya to occur in sadhana practice. Working in the outside world will exhaust the samskaras which cause this unconscious state to arise. Samskaras tend to clog the mind and prevent clarity. Through karma yoga and interacting with other people and life in general, one recognizes and eventually removes one's problems. By doing karma yoga one is able to cross the barrier of unconsciousness in higher sadhana – the 'abyss of death'. When the mind has been harmonized and purged of gross phobias, problems, neuroses, then awareness can be maintained to cross the sea of laya, unconsciousness. After this point is reached in sadhana, the sadhaka will start to explore the superconscious realms of being.

Gaining 'immortality through vidya' means that the 'valley of death' has been crossed, the tendency to become unconscious in meditation. Then the awareness is expanded to an unlimited degree. One is able to transcend the fetters of existence and eventually merge into a state of samadhi, the state of immortality, beyond the limitations of the mind.

Verse 11 contains the essence of spiritual life. It emphasizes that the serious spiritual aspirant should be both extroverted and introverted, practising sadhana or watching the process of the mind to develop inner awareness, while simultaneously working in the world to resolve any mental and emotional problems. This is the sadhana of light, where ida is balanced with pingala. This sadhana of light leads to the rising of kundalini within sushumna, and to spiritual awakening.

The path of light, *devayana*, and the path of darkness, *pitriyana*, are also mentioned in the *Bhagavad Gita* (8:23 onwards), where they are called the northern and southern paths of the Sun. It has the same profound implications. In the *Prashna Upanishad*, the sage Pippalada gives a similar analogy and the same message in response to a question by his disciple Kabandhi. Many other scriptures discuss the same theme.

Work or inner knowledge

If a person has a pair of hands, a pair of legs and good health, how is it possible not to work? Many people are misguided in thinking that if they want illumination or to tread the spiritual path, then they should stop work, or perhaps reduce the workload and be solely concerned with the inner workings of the mind and sit for long hours of sadhana. Many teachers hold the opinion that work, *karma*, and knowledge are mutually exclusive; that if one wants illumination, then one will have to leave all work and practise sadhana day and night. All these ideas are totally wrong and have arisen through a misinterpretation of the scriptures and the sages. Not only is this concept of sadhana wrong, but if followed it will lead to frustration, lack of progress and blockages on the spiritual path. Those who practise unbroken sadhana before they are ready are overcome by desires if they remain in seclusion. Therefore, the important rule is not to remain alone with the impure or lower mind. Many people have made this mistake and are still making this mistake. So ensure the sadhana includes some form of physical action.

This misconception about work, like many misunderstandings, has arisen through the inadequacy of words to define more subtle implications, and the fact that words can be interpreted in different ways according to individual feelings and dogmas. The Sanskrit word for work is karma. Many of the ancient texts clearly state that karma does not lead to illumination, but here karma does not mean work as such; it means rituals and worship performed without feeling or awareness. This type of karma will not lead to illumination, only dullness and ignorance.

The word karma also means any kind of work that is done blindly and instinctively, without awareness. This will lead nowhere on the path of sadhana. One should not stop working but rather continue to work, to do karma, while at the same time trying to maintain awareness. This is achieved by the aspiration and wakefulness of the individual. Awareness during work is also slowly intensified by doing prescribed yogic

128

techniques such as asana, pranayama, meditation practices, bhakti yoga and so forth.

To maintain balance of ida and pingala, it is necessary to combine karma yoga with dhyana yoga. Continuing to act in the world is essential for spiritual awakening, but the work and actions should be done with as much awareness as possible. Work is the means to recognize problems, and it also helps to express and remove them. Do not think of rejecting work or action, but remain detached and transform mere work into karma yoga. Try not to be affected by the ups and downs of work, and do not stop working.

The subject of work and action combined with meditation is one of the main themes of the *Bhagavad Gita*. It constantly emphasizes that actions should never be renounced, only their fruits and attachment to actions and work should be renounced. The *Bhagavad Gita* urges the spiritual aspirant to work according to the dictates of *dharma*, one's natural role in life, but at the same time to try to become more aware of the inner psychic world through meditation practice in sadhana. In this sense, the *Bhagavad Gita* is really discussing the balance of ida and the pingala, without actually mentioning them by name.

The importance of action and work in spiritual sadhana is clearly illustrated by the following experience. Before being initiated as a swami I used to lapse into a state of unconsciousness; I could never go past this state of laya. Eventually

I went to seek the guidance of my guru, Swami Sivananda. The first thing he told me was, "You have to work hard in order to work out your samskaras." He could have said, "Go to a quiet place and practise sadhana for a few years," but he did not. He said, "Work hard," for he knew it was the only way to resolve inner disharmony. Swami Sivananda knew that meditative practices have to be balanced by external action, that ida and pingala have to be balanced. The mind has to be opened up and purified through both karma yoga and meditative practices.

In the ashram a person is expected to work throughout the day. This is not to provide cheap labour for the ashram or for the ashram upkeep, for there are many other people available and willing to do the work necessary for the smooth functioning of the ashram. One is expected to work for one's own sake, for one's spiritual progress. Work is one of the most important aspects of ashram life. It is important in gradually purifying the mind, especially in the early stages of spiritual life.

Many aspirants want to completely absorb themselves in sadhana practice, ceasing to take an active part in the world and often retiring to a quiet retreat. Many sincere and genuine sadhakas have done this for years and have achieved nothing, apart from frustration and disillusionment. They have followed only the ida path, failing to gain the illumination in sadhana they so desperately wanted. They did not realize that illumination cannot come until the karmas have been worked out. All the emotions which have been avoided and suppressed need to come out. The karma which was holding up one's evolution will have to be worked out. The inherent desires and ambitions have to be exhausted and expressed, otherwise they merely remain in a dormant state in the mind as barriers between one's present state of existence and the absolute experience.

One's karma, destiny, personality, one's own self have be faced. The boundary of the body has to be crossed, and then the boundaries of the senses, mind, emotions, intellect and psyche. There are checkpoints. When crossing the boundary of the body, there is a startling experience, and one is thrown back. Of course, there are gurus throughout the world who have the capacity to awaken spiritual experiences, but the problem is that most sadhakas are not able to handle those experiences. Therefore, gurus go slowly. There should be no complacency on the path of sadhana.

Everyone must face fear; there is no use avoiding it. In as much as happiness, comfort, pleasure, love, compassion and charity are wanted, so unhappiness, agony, death, separation, undesirable events, fears, destruction, devastation and so on must be accepted. This can only be done by interacting and working in the world, by following the principles of karma yoga to the best of one's ability. This is the means to clean the mind of its latent problems. It is the pingala aspect.

At the same time a sadhaka should also follow the path of ida, by trying to be aware while working and acting, and by trying to expand inner awareness through meditation practices. This is the way to spiritual unfoldment, not becoming a hermit and rejecting the world.

The path of the wise

The sadhanas of all great illumined sages, saints and yogis have a common pattern; they always combined inner knowledge of the mind with outer actions. Though they had spiritual illumination they still continued to express themselves in the external world, working while maintaining inner awareness. This is the difference between the average aspirant and the sage. The average sadhaka acts without awareness, while the adept keeps a continual flow of awareness. Most people perform actions with little or no awareness. The sage acts, giveing expression to his individuality while maintaining awareness of the totality. In his sadhana he merges the logically opposite aspects of individuality and universality, of action and inaction, of Shiva and Shakti.

Many well-known sages illustrate the common principle of balance and harmony in spiritual sadhana. Christ was illumined, yet he continued to act in the world. He taught his disciples, apostles and followers and travelled all over Galilee. He acted with total awareness. St Teresa was an illumined saint, but she did not stop working; she did more and more work and urged her followers to do the same. Kabir was an illumined bhakta, but he continued to earn his living by weaving and expressed his illumination through his ecstatic songs. These people lived both in the world and beyond the world, combining these two seemingly contradictory modes of being.

Buddha was illumined, but he did not stop acting in the world. He is usually depicted sitting in padmasana or sometimes lying on one side, but this does not mean that he remained motionless like a corpse after his illumination under the bodhi tree in Gaya. Had he done so, the system of Buddhism would never have arisen. His compassion compelled him to teach. Furthermore, he urged his disciples to teach the dharma to others; he instructed them to work for the good of all.

Mohammed was a husband and a father with many duties. He was an active man, but amidst his external activities he expanded his inner knowledge. He was illumined in a cave on Mount Hira. He continued working, but combined his work with awareness, balancing the ida and pingala aspects of his being. Krishna and Rama were both active. In the *Bhagavad Gita*, Krishna urges Arjuna time and time again to know the meaning of action within inaction, to be totally aware while acting with intensity. Krishna did not tell Arjuna to escape from the battlefield at Kurukshetra and go to the Himalayas to meditate and practise austerities. Arjuna was told to fight, but with awareness.

Ramana Maharshi was illumined and although he never did very much intense work, he taught and guided his disciples working in the ashram that grew up around him, preparing food and so forth. Swami Sivananda was the same. He did not stop work, but continued to express himself in many different ways, from writing books to working in the ashram.

Endless examples could be given of other sages who continued to act in the world as part and parcel of their sadhana. There seem to be no exceptions; their sadhanas were a combination of inner illumination with work in the world, with awareness of the underlying nature of everything. Their sadhana integrated the realm of the phenomenal and relative, or *samsara*, with the transcendental, or *nirvana*. They combined the limited with the unlimited. They acted as a crossroad between the finite and the infinite, the temporal and the eternal. Their sadhana balanced the inner with the outer.

Follow the example of these illumined sages. Do not reject work. Change the attitude to work, try to be more detached, renounce the fruits mentally and be aware, but do not stop. If one is lost and totally involved in external actions, as are most aspirants, then take steps to unfold the inner awareness. Start to practise sadhana. On the other hand, if there is excessive introversion with a tendency to brood over problems and deficiencies, then try to take more interest in the outside world. Do intense one-pointed work, but try to be aware at the same time. There should be balance between ida and pingala. Follow the example of the wise, for this is the way to open up the potential and understanding of what sadhana really is.

Practise sadhana and live the divine life

In spiritual sadhana there should be a continual process of adjustment. Awareness of the inner world is expanded and from this the relationships and understanding of the outside world are adjusted. It is a continual process of synchronizing the ida and pingala principles so that they are always balanced.

Living a life of inner disharmony will create trouble. Practising sadhana and living for a higher purpose means organizing the patterns of one's own life. Many times people try to maintain a yoga sadhana while going to bed late at night and waking up late in the morning; the same applies to their diet and all other aspects of their personal life. If there is no system, discipline and order in life, one may still be a good person but will not be in harmony with oneself because one is living a life of paradoxes.

133

12

Aids to Success in Sadhana

The most difficult of all sadhana practices is where the aspirant realizes and sees His mysterious role behind all trials and tribulations. Trials and tribulations are but forms of His grace. They serve as a barometer to indicate the seriousness and grossness of the imperfect personality. Without trying conditions, one could not gauge one's personality. Samskaras of the past have to be burned; disease, discomfort, disturbance, insult, unpleasant situations all help to purge foreign matter from the soul. This is the meaning of purification. God creates every event with a great purpose behind it. Wise people do not oppose it, for they know His mission. Know this truth very well: that praise and appreciation and love and recognition will only stand in the way of spiritual progress.

If an aspirant is sincere in his practices, he will definitely come across obstacles created by the mind, which are a natural outcome of the mind's entry into spiritual life. There will be times when one may face disillusionment and waver in one's convictions. This is especially true for those who, in spite of long and arduous practice, fail to have any sustaining inner experience. The ultimate experience may then start to be regarded as a myth. After all, it remains an abstract phenomenon until it becomes a living reality.

Do not expect to be bright, cheerful, optimistic and full of faith and devotion at all times. It is impractical and unrealistic to think along these lines. If there is no success in attaining any substantial experience, one may curtail the practices due to misgivings and lack of inspiration. At such times, if there is no one at hand to inspire and reaffirm one's convictions, one may feel dejected and full of despair. This can happen to any aspirant at any time. It is a natural outcome of the spiritual journey.

Do not be fooled at any step of the journey. Indecision, disbelief and lack of inspiration are integral parts of existence and one has to learn to cope with all these conditions without letting them have an adverse effect. If one's convictions and beliefs are facing a severe trial, try to learn from that situation too. Strive to cope with anything that comes in a positive, peaceful and uplifting manner. When the clouds of doubt are washed away, one will find greater fulfilment in the sadhana that has been undertaken. The ways and means to revive the inspiration have to be found. One of the most readily available, useful and constructive methods is *swadhyaya*, self-study or self-analysis through the scriptures.

Natural purging

On the spiritual path an aspirant is involuntarily subjected to a purging process. Just as shankhaprakshalana is practised to cleanse the physical body, in the same way consciousness has to be purged of its animal tendencies, the experiences of instinctive life. They are always there, but during the course of sadhana they manifest in the form of jealousy, anger, greed, passion, desires, guilt, distractions and so on. They seem to be obstacles but they are not; they are nature's way of purging the dirt. This process is always going on, but as one proceeds further in spiritual life, this purging might become so acute that it smells foul and one feels very bad about oneself, dirty, repulsive and completely hopeless. The aspirant says, "What terrible things I am thinking. Oh God! I do not want all this." These are not obstacles; they must be understood as part of the process of transformation, and the reason why sadhana needs to be practised.

135

When some type of sickness arises while practising sadhana, it must be understood firstly that one is working out the process of one's karma. Sickness indicates the expulsion of impurities from the body. Expelling toxic matter is the first law of nature. Sickness also leads to an appreciation that there is something wrong somewhere in the pattern of one's daily life, either in the realm of thinking or in the realm of eating or habits. Remember that days of sickness are days of blessings. During sickness, when the mind becomes calm and quiet, there is no passion, no fantasy and all the turbulence subsides. Sickness can bring serenity of mind.

Alertness, vigilance, receptivity

One has to be ever alert and constant in both practice and aspiration. Even if the whole world collapses around the aspirant, it does not matter. A spiritual experience can occur at any moment and one has to be prepared to sustain it on every level. It is not just something which happens to the spirit and leaves the body and mind unaffected. If one gives up hope and effort, one can never be successful.

The divine power is gracious to devotees and disguises itself in many forms just to test their devotion and faith. When the aspirant gives up hope and belief because the odds seem to have turned against him, he has misunderstood the situation. Due to concepts of good and bad one assumes that a particular experience is negative and reacts to it. However, whether circumstances seem to be pleasant or unpleasant, one must maintain faith and continue one's practice; only then can sadhana bear fruit.

A sadhaka remains poised and ever ready for an event which will occur inevitably in its own time. He accepts that to precipitate that event is not within his control or power, yet it is his destiny that it will occur and he must be ever vigilant in sadhana. It should not be interpreted as fatalism or laziness, but as a state of surrender and readiness which is to be sustained by constant awareness. That is why in yoga, relaxation is a sattwic experience, not a tamasic one. Relaxation for

136

a sadhaka is not inertia, indolence, laziness or 'turning off'. Rather it is a state of equipoise, balance and receptivity.

Six enemies

The six foes of the sadhaka are: lust, greed, anger, sensual hypnosis, pride or arrogance, and envy or jealousy. These aspects of the personality will definitely be encountered as they are inherently ingrained in the human psyche. They become particularly strong at the moment of spiritual awakening and reveal a type of mental deformity in an otherwise sensible individual. They become the enemies of every spiritual aspirant, taking away the peace and harmony of life, extroverting the awareness and making it gross. They are the causes of mental distraction and dissipation as they disrupt the flow of energy of the mind and divert the inner attention from the goal. They do not allow one to focus and to go deep into the practices so that spiritual awakening can take place.

If spiritual sadhana does not allow one to conquer these six obstructions, there can be no evolution. One may enjoy meditation or other practices, but that is not the point of sadhana. The only way to overcome these enemies is to have an overwhelming desire to be rid of these impurities. The distraction, dissipation and agitation caused by envy, lust, anger, greed, pride and sensual hypnosis will need to be removed by the regular practice of asana, pranayama, japa, meditation, prayer, etc. Karma yoga will help expose this side of oneself and will also help to conquer it. The sadhana should act upon the causes of mental and emotional disturbances and lead to an irrevocable peace within.

During the spiritual ascent, both negative and positive experiences are part of the cleansing process. When experiencing them, one is passing through what is called 'purgatory'. It is a natural process. Let it happen. Once the spiritual path has been chosen, no matter what obstacles are met, the sadhaka must continue towards his goal and not retrace his steps for any reason. Looked at objectively, obstacles are actually stepping stones. Any mistake provides experience so that

137

when the same obstacle is met again, one will know how to deal with it.

Distractions are natural and to gain success in sadhana the aspirant will need to learn to live in the world without being affected by it. Even if living in seclusion on the top of a mountain, or isolating oneself in a soundproof chamber, there will still be distractions. Distractions are born of desires, ignorance and unawareness of the spirit, aspects of the lower mind. When the inner path is not being followed side by side with external life, there will be more distractions, whether living in the country or in a busy city.

Rechannel all the diffused and confused patterns of consciousness into the central focus of sadhana. Make sadhana the objective to be achieved. It should form the object of meditation, the only thing to be known and to be worshipped, the only object of bliss. Be confident of attaining perfection in sadhana.

Fearlessness

Everybody wants immortality, nobody wants death. Death causes fear. People cannot face it, or even think about it. What is reality? Is it happiness, love, compassion or charity? Fear is reality, agony is reality, disease is reality. No one wants to face it, but it will come out in one's sadhana practices, because this toxic matter has been accumulating in the mental system for thirty, forty or fifty years. Unless it is faced squarely, the aspirant cannot have higher experiences.

Read the lives of great saints who had illumination. What a life St Francis faced! It is impossible to be realized and go further in sadhana without being able to undergo suffering, insult and criticism. Those who are cowardly, who have no independence of thought, who have no high aim or goal in life, will never be able to remedy their defects or make progress in sadhana. How can a person who is afraid of man-made difficulties, ever-changing beliefs and foolish sentiments stay in unearthly, imperishable and luminous realms? The prime necessity for a sadhaka is to have self-confidence and be above influences. It is desirable and beneficial for the sadhaka to be concerned with the present and never have the slightest intellectual confusion.

Fear is always an imaginary belief, a hindrance to personality, and in this world no one is free from the influence of fear. Be fearless, cowards never acquire the power of life. Proceed in sadhana only if fear can be fully shed. A person who is afraid of a fly will never be able to pass by the lion's den. Fear breaks the organized pattern of the mind which is formed in continuous sadhana. Fear weakens willpower. The impressions of fear are obstructions to the awakening of kundalini, and what can a sadhaka who is ready to awaken higher conscious gain from being afraid? So long as fear exists, one's willpower will not function and bear fine fruits.

How to become fearless? Secret talks, letters, relationships and affairs all give birth and strength to fear complexes, and as long as there is something that needs to be hidden from others, one will continue to be afraid. So never indulge in things that need to be hidden from others. This is a sure aid to success in spiritual life. In the beginning it may be a little difficult, but by and by everything will become possible.

When one has taken to the spiritual path, all of these obstacles and more should be expected to arise because one is not yet perfect. Until then the imperfect mind will be with the aspirant and it is this mind which will create obstacles. All obstacles are offspring of the mind, and until the mind is purified obstacles will continue on one's path, whatever it might be. Always try to feel the highest bliss and peace. Gradually try to develop an atmosphere of peace on the psychic level. It is the function of the mind to worry; its root lies in fear. It is not the attribute of the soul, for that is changeless.

The mind of a sadhaka is the *kalpataru*; it has the ability to materialize what is desired. The feelings arising in the ocean of the mind become converted into spiritual power. If the mind is full of faith, fearlessness, hope and goodness, the sadhaka receives infinite boons. If he becomes frightened in

139

adverse conditions and loses that precious faith, he is lost and doomed. Always be humble. A weary traveller sat under the shade of a kalpataru tree to rest. He wished for some water, for he was very thirsty, and wonder of wonders, he got water to drink. Then he thought of sleeping. Lo, he got a fine bed to sleep in. In the evening, when he looked around the wild forest, he became frightened of the forest animals. Lo, a tiger came and devoured him!

Discipline

Discipline is the backbone of sadhana. It is of two kinds, organizational and personal. Personal discipline is essential for spiritual progress in the same way as organizational discipline is necessary for the progress of society and the nation. Just as a country with a disciplined army has no fears, similarly, the aspirant who has disciplined the senses is guaranteed success. How can the destination be reached when the horses of the chariot have no reins and the driver is restless? An alert driver, who is clear about his destiny and able to command and steer his senses, is bound to attain his goal. By maintaining the discipline of regular practice, control over the body and mind can be achieved. The real goal lies within oneself.

Pride and ego

Real sadhana begins when the aspirant realizes that he is separate from God, that he is His servant, or whatever other relationship has been developed. Prior to that, sublimation, elimination or total destruction of the ego is necessary. This feeling of 'I am the doer' has to be destroyed. There is vanity, egoism, mean-mindedness and a lot of pride within the average person and during the practice of sadhana many of these symptoms will manifest. At some stage he will probably think, 'I am a sadhaka and all these other people are wretched.' A lot of mental dissipations, oscillations and distractions will also have to be faced. One will have to face them all. They should be recognized and not opposed, and then they will go away in the course of time.

140

Remember that sadhana is a gradual process of self-purification. Selflessness does not come all of a sudden; it is the culmination of the total process of sadhana. The obstacles confronted in the beginning are inevitable, but if the practices are continued with the attitude of a detached witness, the ego will definitely fade away. One's sadhana may at times become weak and sometimes one naturally becomes impatient. Even though there may have been progress on the path of sadhana, this lack of contentment may continue until final fulfilment is reached. Such discontentment is healthy.

Avoid self-assessment

It is not for the aspirant to maintain the balance sheet of his sadhana. His duty is to go on practising it. A basic mental weakness of a sadhaka is anxiety to know whether he is progressing in sadhana or not. Do not be in a hurry to assess the measure of success in meditation, nor to analyze experiences in sadhana. So long as the form of the ishta cannot be experienced within in full measure, do not think about achievements. Herein lies the weakness of sadhakas. They continue to progress and yet continue to measure the way traversed.

Remember that when success on the spiritual path is achieved, instead of being conscious of the measure of his progress, the sadhaka, remains conscious only of the form of his ishta or of devotion to Him. So long as an aspirant continues to remain conscious of his success, the ultimate reality will remain far away. Therefore, one should not be restless, nor should one shape oneself according to other people's assessments. Remain indifferent to praise and blame. Do not be receptive to criticism.

What is wrong if the speed is slow? An ant carrying a small piece of grain was trying to climb a wall. It fell down twenty times, but on the twenty-first attempt the ant succeeded in climbing the wall with that little piece of grain. There are emotional ups and downs. Sometimes there is confusion and depression. Often faith in one's own self is lost, but again it must be regained. Never lose courage.

141

A life devoted to sadhana should not defeat the aspirant, nor should problems destroy him. Loss of property, death of the nearest and dearest, betrayal by the best friend, nothing should make one lose heart. The future of those who remain excited and restless is dark indeed. Everybody has an infinite chance to improve, and there is not just one life. There is not just one chance but infinite chances.

Introversion and extroversion

At a particular stage of evolution, a sadhaka becomes very extroverted, which does not mean that he is given to sensual life, but that he becomes aware of everything which is outside and can be received or understood by the senses. People whose senses are extroverted can reach this spiritual point more easily and quickly than introverted people. Those who are introverted by nature will have to externalize their sensory perceptions, develop them, make them keener and more sensitive, and then introvert them.

Introversion is a spiritual disqualification in sadhana. In the ashram aspirants who are spontaneously introverted by nature are not allowed to do a lot of meditation, because they do not know how to manipulate or manage the mind. If the mind dives deep when a lot of meditation and japa is being done, there must be the capacity to bring it back. Therefore, the mind should not be introverted unless it is first externalized. Introversion is neurotic behaviour.

Spiritual insight or spiritual awareness is quickly available to a person who is extroverted by nature. People who are introverted by nature will find it very difficult to maintain the continuous flow of awareness required during meditation. Therefore, in yoga and in ashram life, people who are introverted by nature have the scope of their sensory activities awakened and widened through the practice of karma yoga.

Overcoming samskaras

Visions which appear and disappear during meditation are the forms of samskaras. If they are not removed, the object of meditation will not be realized. Just as the sun is covered by clouds and things are concealed in darkness, likewise consciousness of one's self is covered by samskaras. In order to revive the consciousness of the higher self, the samskaras have to be removed, for which total awareness and strong determination are required.

Samskaras and habits constitute the principal impediments in yoga sadhana. One who tries to reach the heights of sadhana without overcoming the samskaras will certainly have to return. Only those who have attained both *viveka*, discrimination, and *vairagya*, dispassion, are able to overcome all the collected impressions of past lives. For one who is detached and who has discrimination, who is established in the awareness that 'I am neither the doer nor the enjoyer', even the present actions cause no obstructions.

The sixfold virtues are methods of removing the obstructions of the samskaras. The sadhaka who has been able to overcome all the obstructions of the samskaras will have an unobstructed passage, and will attain the ultimate union, *yoga*. The sixfold virtues, known as *shadsampat*, are: *shama*, calming the sense organs; *dama*, restraining the senses; *uparati*, withdrawing from the senses, or pratyahara; *titiksha*, endurance; *shraddha*, faith in the words of the guru and in the existence of God; and *samadhana*, mental balance, which is the result of the practice and realization of shama, dama, uparati, titiksha and shraddha. A spiritual aspirant should also posses *mumukshutva*, an intense desire for liberation. These attributes should be applied in spiritual practice and in daily life.

Become a witness
Another condition for success in sadhana is detachment. A spiritual aspirant is born into the world and survives by the world, because without the world there is no sadhana. But at the same time, do not be of the world. Be the observer. Let things keep coming, but try to remain above them all. Nothing should injure one's mind. Let the body live in the world; let the mind rest in consciousness. Be free from affectations.

143

Thus the mind will never become disturbed by the pairs of opposites, which will make it steady enough to receive and maintain the light of concentration. This type of mental detachment will redouble the force of sadhana.

Through sadhana try to practise being an impartial spectator. Learn to withdraw the attachment from mundane affairs, which is the process of vairagya, and then merge the same in God-consciousness, which is abhyasa. The mind, which is naturally inclined towards petty objects and pleasures, should be brought back every time it loses touch with the centre. The thoughts which naturally follow the twin trends of attraction and repulsion, *raga* and *dwesha*, will have to be turned and led towards the seat of the Supreme.

That practice takes time to develop; it is not so easy that it can be started from today. It is not simply a matter of just saying, "No, I am not related to you; I am not attached to you." One is related to everybody – father, mother, sister, brother and cousin, but there are things which damage the mind and completely destroy the mental structure from time to time. Every aspirant has to be very careful because one cannot proceed inside with a damaged mind. So take care of the mind. The path of sadhana must be plain, smooth and simple. Spare no effort. Do not care for success and failure. Take care of mental equilibrium. Remain as a witness.

Spiritualize experiences and perceptions

If the sadhaka seeks happiness, rest and light in the higher self alone, then neither desire nor infatuation nor attachment will obstruct him in the quest. It is not correct to say that the highest state of realization is achieved only by giving up all connections with the natural functioning of the mind and the senses. Waiting for such a stage in sadhana will lead to disappointment for ages. The flow of the sentiments will have to be diverted towards the light of *chidakasha*, the inner space of consciousness, and knowledge of *Brahman*, the ultimate reality. The ideals will have to be changed and the sentiments, experiences and perceptions spiritualized.

It is not necessary to kill desire. It is also unnecessary to break off all relationships, or to suppress aversion. It is not necessary to fight against these troubles. On the contrary, make them divine and then it will be realized that the stream of *vasanas*, subtle desires, is flowing rapidly towards that *maha yajna*, supreme sacrifice. There may then be a feeling of disgust, but that is due to ignorance. There will be relations only with one's fixed ideals. There will be attachment only for one's ishta. There will be greed only to perform selfless service. Discontentment will be due to indolence in sadhana. In this way, without destroying them, the senses and their functions can be used for the maha yajna.

One has to know the trick of acquiring detachment and spiritualization. Do not be influenced either by thoughts of imagined faults and weaknesses, or greatness. On the contrary, take frequent flights into chidakasha and meet the *purusha*, the supreme being, often and again. Then the totality of one's activities will gain the experience of unity or oneness, even though on the surface one will appear to be a worldly person. This is the inner trick, which has no connection with the intellect or books. It is only a matter of subtle understanding.

Dedicate every act

No one need change their status or vocation in life, nor their duties. All that is necessary is to perform sadhana in order to awaken the secret power of yoga, which is within. In other words, every idea and every act should be dedicated with single-minded devotion to sadhana. It is most important to keep the mind fully occupied so that it cannot find the time to wander here and there. A fully occupied life helps in dwelling within. Try steadily to go in through the practices of inner silence, shavasana, ajapa japa and ishta sadhana. Apart from these, know that there is a divine purpose behind whatever one is doing.

Convert all the daily actions into sadhana. Be constantly aware that one is not the body, the prana, the mind, the antahkarana, a collection of sense organs, emotions, desires, karma and samskaras, but a wonderful element of prakriti; and yet transcending all these, one is also a treasure house of marvellous things. If this awareness can be kept constant, the sadhana will move into a new dimension, the field of inner consciousness will open up, the form of devotion, the form of concentration and meditation will appear before the sadhaka in each and every person, place and event in life.

The main concern is sadhana

It is not possible for a sadhaka to be totally free from ignorance. Ignorance persists in some measure, however small, until the final fulfilment is reached. But remember that in spite of obstacles, there is progress. Perfection will be attained if one does not give up. Let no event of the world influence the inner spirit and make one despondent or elated. Ensure by any means that the efforts of years are not reduced to nothing in a second, and that the sadhana of lifetimes is not undone in a minute. People feel ruined by slander and bloated by flattery; they fall by failure and are blinded by success.

Every movement of life is His projection and all activities, both inside and outside the world, are carried out within that projection. The inner temple has to be reached. Do not bother about faults. The main concern of a sadhaka is his sadhana. One who concerns himself with other matters cannot succeed in sadhana. One who is fond of sweetness, subject to infatuation and influences, forever attached, is not a sadhaka.

Hankering after praise and seeking one's own advantage will halt progress. For the path of sadhana is open to those who are indifferent to the world, who remain absorbed or are sublime lovers. Know that there is the infinite power of yoga within. Awaken this power by regular, constant, continuous and sincere efforts in sadhana. If there is extreme intensity, real love, indomitable will and a deep abiding thirst for absolute knowledge, there is no power on earth which can create a hindrance on this path.

There should be no hard and fast rule while doing sadhana. Adjust the sadhana. Use commonsense. Never get excited about one's sadhana. Excitement brings about depression and consequently fatigue. Keeping a cool head and a balanced mind and being efficient in one's duties is a sadhana in itself.

Be happy and cheerful, and allow life to be joyful. Become an incarnation of happiness. Cast off all mental and physical burdens. Work hard. Do not waste a single moment in laziness, brooding, dreaming, worrying and weeping. Doubts do arise in every mind. Why did God make this world? What is the use of sadhana when even a leaf cannot move without His orders? Lead a proper life while practising sadhana and adjusting with the family environment. Side by side, keep the light of the atman alive in every atom of the being.

A true sadhaka feels His grace and mercy when tempests try to move him. The strongest sadhaka thanks all of them because they come to judge and confirm his strength. Abuse, insults, injuries, taunts, harassment and discomforts have strengthened my personality. Let me repeat my mantra, which my guru whispered into my soul, "Adapt, adjust, accommodate; bear insult, bear injury; highest sadhana."

13

Seclusion and Sadhana

Going into seclusion is like sending a car to the workshop and not using it for a while. When the car needs overhauling, the machine is left to cool down, each part is cleaned and lubricated and then the car is taken for a test run on side roads. When it is certain that the brakes work properly and everything is in order, the car can then be taken on the main road or freeway. In the same way, the mind, the body, the senses and maybe all the other parts that are unknown need a thorough repair and overhaul.

How does the aspirant know when an overhaul is necessary? When mental and psychic impurities are coming up without being wanted, when something feels wrong with the body despite eating well and there is a feeling of exhaustion. When the body, mind and senses are in poor condition, the wisest thing to do, even for an ordinary person, is to go into seclusion for a period of time, to send the car to the workshop for repair. If the owner wants the car to be not only repaired but made fully automatic as well, it will take more time. The manufacturers will need to install new parts and so the car has to stay longer at the workshop. For normal purposes, fifteen days of complete seclusion will do. Anyone can try it and it will make a great difference to their health, both physical and mental. For higher spiritual purposes, there should be a longer period of silence and seclusion.

Some people retire to a quiet place and start to practise sadhana. However, this method is only for those who do not have too many inner conflicts or strong ties with the world. Few people can do this, for most have responsibilities and no great urge to leave the busy world anyway. Furthermore, it is not necessary to become a hermit to practise sadhana; continue the daily activities and practise karma yoga. In both cases, living in solitude or in bustling surroundings, it is necessary to develop a sense of renunciation in order to gain the most from all yogic practices.

If a person retires to a cave with an outward renunciation of the world, but with a deep inward longing for worldly objects and enjoyments, then he is fooling himself and will make no progress in sadhana. This is not renunciation, for he is still very attached. The path for most people is in and through the world while practising sadhana.

When kundalini awakens

It is said that Christ was tempted by Satan; and Mara, or the devil, came to Buddha and troubled him throughout the night of his enlightenment. From the yogic point of view, these references describe the stage after the awakening of enlightenment, when samskaras and karmas quickly burst out. Passion, anger, greed, ego, attachment, vanity, pride, jealousy, neurosis, fear of death and many other things may appear. For this reason it is recommended that when the awakening begins, until there is stability, the aspirant should cut himself off and go into seclusion; otherwise he will create chaos, abuse everybody and do all kinds of strange things. That is also the rule when there is awakening of kundalini.

149

The sadhaka should go into seclusion and minimize worldly activities.

When kundalini awakens, sadhakas need such a place where the atmosphere is pure, and they can meditate all day without being disturbed either emotionally, mentally, physically or spiritually. Such places can be found in the Himalayas, particularly in the areas of Gangotri, Uttarkashi, Badrinath and Kedarnath. These are the four places where rishis and gurus live in absolute seclusion for many centuries in calm and quiet samadhi. The spiritual energy generated by them is so powerful that it even affects the physical ecology.

Seclusion with a spiritual purpose

Retiring into seclusion with a spiritual purpose is intended to avoid unwanted and unnecessary associations with society. Sadhakas retire into seclusion to avoid these distractions and to practise higher sadhana earnestly. The advantages of seclusion for spiritual practice are supreme. However, for success in this stage of sadhana one must have the blessings of the guru before undertaking it.

Seclusion is not a practice, but a means of creating a powerful atmosphere in order to practise sadhana. For example,

150

one may decide to do ten million repetitions of Gayatri mantra in so many days; that is a sadhana. Silence and seclusion are the arrangements one makes in order to keep the body, mind and senses free from the disturbances which are unavoidable in society.

Even someone who is not spiritually evolved will make quick progress by going into seclusion under the guidance of a guru with a definite program. When a sadhaka is in seclusion for many years without meeting anyone, if he is a sincere aspirant, the world becomes almost non-existent. In seclusion and silence one is nearer to oneself. All the values are lost and the subconscious mind becomes very powerful. All the things usually seen in life can be seen within.

Attitudes to seclusion

If an aspirant is very keen about self-realization, at some time sadhana must be practised in seclusion, in absolute silence. However, it must be complete seclusion, where there is enough time to see oneself and at the same time one is not compelled to see other people. Some sadhus retire from their homes and have a house in Rishikesh and another in Gangotri or Haridwar. They have a servant who cooks for them and a bank account. They go shopping and choose their vegetables, and sometimes if a mahatma comes to the district, they visit him. This is not seclusion.

It is also said in the *Bhagavad Gita* that one should try to enjoy seclusion and keep away from the company of anyone. The elders have made rules and they must be followed. Every field of life has its own set of regulations, and sadhana is no exception. Seclusion means cooking one's own food and trying to avoid the company of other people as much as possible. The socializing tendencies of the mind to meet people and exchange greetings must be checked.

I spent nine months in Gangotri. One day I went to see a mahatma. He was sitting quietly and I waited, expecting him to call me, but he did not. After a while I said, "I have just arrived here." He said, "Don't waste your time here. Go back to your own place. I am not interested in you." This is the sort of attitude one must have in seclusion. Such mahatmas never meet anyone. There was another very old mahatma, and when people used to come to Gangotri on pilgrimage, his disciples would carry him higher up the mountain until they left.

Readiness for seclusion

During periods of seclusion, the reactions of each sadhaka take place according to the individual's stage of evolution, and it is hard to generalize. Some spiritual aspirants are all right as long as they are in society, but the moment they retire into seclusion, fear creeps in. All kinds of insecurities and passions come into the mind. They become so confused and afraid that they come out of seclusion and go back into society. One sadhaka went to Gangotri, high up in the mountains. He used to eat potatoes and khichari once a day. Suddenly he felt that his whole spinal cord was full of heat, and visions of all dimensions came to him. He was aware of the outer world and the inner visions at the same time, and he could not manage it. He thought perhaps he had gone mad and he had to leave.

During a long period of seclusion, a sadhaka may be able to practise higher sadhana uninterrupted. He can get up easily at two am and practise sadhana up to eight o'clock. Then he perhaps takes a little walk and rests and starts again at ten o'clock. If the sadhaka is earnest and properly prepared, seclusion gives him so much energy that he can practise sadhana for hours at a time without exhaustion or depression, without any difficulties. However, for the first four or five days, whenever he closes his eyes sleep may overpower him, but after that sleep will gradually be reduced. It might come down to as little as two or three hours a day. Swami Sivananda said that he had so much energy while living a secluded life that he used to chant 'Om' out loud at night. At the dead of night he would stand in the icy cold Ganga, do japa and come back full of energy.

152

In seclusion, the sadhaka must have some kind of program because there is no one to check up on him. Of course, many sadhus go into seclusion without a sadhana and after a few days they cannot stand it any longer. Once I went into seclusion in Rishikesh for three months. I had a program. I knew what to do, japa and dhyana, but still I could not do it. Lethargy and indolence took over because I was not prepared for seclusion. In the morning I would take my mala and go to sleep. When it was nine o'clock I would go to the kshetra for my rotis. Then I would come back, take my *Brahma Sutras*, start one sutra and fall asleep. I would get up at three o'clock, take a bath and again go to the kshetra for rotis. When I came back, I would take my mala and sleep! I knew what I had to do, but I could not do it. I was not ready for this stage of sadhana.

Various stages of sadhana

Seclusion is a stage of sadhana; it depends on the sadhaka. It is not the same for everybody, as it depends upon the state of evolution. Great saints like Christ, Buddha, Mohammed and Mahavira went into seclusion before their self-realization. Much of Christ's life is not recorded, but he did retire for forty days into the wilderness. Buddha retired for some years, and Mohammed and Mahavira went into the mountains.

At various stages of spiritual sadhana one has to act differently. In the beginning of spiritual life, one must try to avoid undesirable associations and deal only with desirable and compulsory associations. Then, when a spiritual aspirant is developing sadhana and doing well, experiencing something within like peace of mind, oneness, concentration, he must compulsorily associate with activities, actions and karmas where for some time his mind and senses are extroverted. It can be any work where the mind is extroverted, like cooking vegetables, gardening or housework or helping a sick person. The association is with external activities, with the action, the work, not with other people. This is not complete solitude, but it is as good as.

Eventually there comes a time, in the case of a very rare sort of sadhaka, when he has to close himself off completely from people, from work, and remain in absolute solitude, do his own sadhana and experience, but that is not for long. Then there again comes a time when one has to relate with every event, with everybody, desirable or undesirable.

Seclusion for paramahamsa sannyasa

Sannyasa has four stages. One is *kutichak*, when a sannyasin lives with his guru for ten to twelve years. The second stage is *parivrajaka*, wandering for ten to twelve years. Then comes *hamsa*, the third stage: opening an ashram, starting a math, erecting a mandir, running an orphanage, opening a hospital.

The fourth stage is *paramahamsa*, which means staying in one place alone, in order to become stable. The paramahamsa lives in solitude and becomes established in Brahman. Having abandoned all attachment and freed himself from the influence of duality, worldly affairs can no longer bind him. Before that stage he can go hither and thither to satsangs and kirtans. A paramahamsa sannyasin no longer plays the role of a guru or makes disciples. There is a time for retirement. In old age, how long can one go on caring for one's children? Blessing malas, giving mantra diksha and so on can be done up to the stage of paramahamsa sannyasa, as long as one is a guru.

No one should prostrate at the feet of a paramahamsa sannyasin, and in solitude theses rules can be followed. When the stage of paramahamsa sannyasa is reached, attending meetings and taking alms are prohibited. Sadhanas or anushthanas, mouna, and worship of God have to be done twenty-four hours of the day. These are the rules.

Advantages of seclusion

Seclusion has many advantages. The physical activity of the brain becomes absolutely calm. Under normal conditions, the vibrations caused by the influx of blood and fluctuating rhythms of the lungs and heat change due to thoughts, physical movement and various kinds of exertion. That is completely avoided in silence and seclusion. The taste for life becomes extremely weak. However, it can be said with absolute authority that even after fifty years of silence and seclusion, everything in life can become weak but not the will of God.

Buddha had to come down to earth and so did Christ, Mahavira and many others. They had to work hard in society before leaving it for a period of higher sadhana in solitude. *Samadhi,* union with the divine, is a higher sadhana which requires total absorption in the divine. Any transaction with the outside world precludes samadhi. Therefore, it is imperative to wear spiritual armour and prevent worldly interactions from happening. That is why sadhus and mahatmas are allowed to gather people around them for a certain period of time. They can train disciples, run institutions and hospitals, teach yoga, meet people, or have discussions for ten, twenty or fifty years. Then, if they want to evolve into higher consciousness, all these activities must stop. Everyone, not only myself, should retire after such a long period of active selfless service, stay in solitude and refrain from meeting people.

There are other advantages too. In seclusion sadhakas find that the thoughts gradually diminish. Ultimately they may not be at all interested in thinking. It is not that they check the thoughts, but they are just not interested in them. As a result of sadhana, the conscious personality becomes more introverted, and the subconscious personality is expressed in the form of visions and other experiences. One feels quiet, and then ultimately the unconscious personality reveals itself. It is a state of mind that lasts for a certain period of time. In fact, the only way a sadhaka can reveal his unconscious personality is by going into seclusion for a long period, under the guidance of his guru. The emergence of the unconscious is the same as the awakening of samadhi. Ramakrishna Paramahamsa would often be unconscious for six days, sitting in exactly the same position. His disciples had to sing kirtan in front of him, otherwise he would not get up.

Similarly, there was an avadhoota who used to sit by the river in samadhi for days at a stretch. He would not be disturbed or awoken by any sound, even a train passing by. But if two people sat down beside him and began to talk about *Brahma vidya*, the supreme existence, he would immediately open his eyes. His unconscious personality was so conscious of these things that his samadhi would break at once.

Experiences in seclusion

When sadhus practise pranayama in silence and seclusion, different kinds of experiences arise. The senses become so keen that the vibrations of the wind and the direction it is blowing in can be sensed from inside a room. If a bird makes a sound, even in the dead of night, it can be heard from a distance of two or three miles. The sense of smell becomes sharp enough to tell when the mahatma living half a mile away puts water on the fire to boil potatoes.

The sense of sight may also become more developed. At night, when looking out of the window, how high the snow is far away and which stone has been submerged can be seen. Whatever the mind thinks of can become like a movie, as if images form by themselves. Once when I was performing sadhana in seclusion, I was thinking about the mythological descent of Ganga, and the image came to me so clearly that I could actually see a man with broad shoulders, King Bhagirath, and the flow of water falling on him. It was not a thought but a vision in the form of a true image.

That is the effect of silence and seclusion. The mind has a great capacity, but in society the mental energy is used up in many ways, moment to moment. People are so accustomed to using a lot of brainpower without realizing it because it seems to require no effort. It is like playing a tape recorder when the battery is flat. Insufficient energy is being received. That same mental energy is conserved during long periods of silence and seclusion. However, there are some people who have found the perennial source of energy and are connected to it. In order to tap that perennial source one must retire into seclusion, otherwise it is not possible.

156

14

Advice on Sadhana

It is important for any serious sadhaka to appreciate, accept and understand his own lifestyle. Human beings are subject to the laws of universal or cosmic nature, and according to those laws each individual has a certain type of personality, way of thinking, conviction or weakness that will influence his sadhana from time to time. One may perform actions full of faults or defects. Side by side the mind may also remain afflicted. This can become a curse in the practice of sadhana, but do not worry about it or try to get out of it. Continue the practices with the understanding that whatever experiences one has already undergone, is going through and will be going through are all a part of one's sadhana, and not detrimental to it.

In the practice of sadhana there is nothing to relinquish or reject. As a person evolves, many habits, addictions and experiences are left behind. The sensualities of life, the infirmities of willpower, habits and weaknesses will all fade away one by one by themselves if effort continues to be put into sadhana. It is no use accepting defeat on the path of sadhana. It is only necessary to perform the sadhana with a direction and to constantly renew one's enthusiasm.

Be alive to sankalpa

A sadhaka must always remember his sankalpa or resolve with determination. The test does not lie in how much sadhana has been practised, but how alive one is to one's sankalpa.

157

Therefore, go on revising all the good resolutions. Take a bird's eye view of oneself moving in and about this life. Remember that it will take some time to go above the plane of sense consciousness. Incessant practice will be necessary.

There should be an obsessive desire to know the highest truth and great reverence for the divine path of sadhana that leads to it. The sadhaka has been given a sadhana by His grace, and it should be constantly upheld. One is expected to be earnest and true to it, and nobody in the world should be able to shatter one's noble faith and convictions.

If one does not miss the objective and is dedicated completely to the fulfilment of one's aim, there will surely be success. Sincerity and surrender are the greatest assets in sadhana. Even if there are a host of defects, concerted effort will certainly overcome them. Divine spirits will help with this effort and lead the aspirant along the path, giving new direction whenever necessary. Always keep the battery charged. Aim and faith alone is first and last in sadhana. Adopt, decide and retain the aim throughout everything. Infuse and express faith sincerely, knowing that certainty about success leads to success. Go forth with confidence, with full conviction and faith that the path of sadhana is correct.

Correct and incorrect sadhana

Some people say that when sadhana is wrongly practised it can be harmful, but nothing wrong can happen because the inner structure of the body has a built-in defence mechanism. Nature has created bumper bars or shock absorbers. If asanas are practised incorrectly or pranayama is overdone, there are signals or symptoms which immediately compel one to stop, if one is sensible and listens to the signals being sent by the body and mind. For example, if breath retention is overdone in the beginning, within a few days strain will be felt and there will be absolutely no desire to practise it. Just as with indigestion there is no desire to eat, similarly, if asanas and pranayama are practised incorrectly, then nature will create a condition in the mind whereby one will not want to practise again unless under expert guidance. If that voice of experience is ignored and the practitioner goes ahead obstinately, then maybe the mind will fuse, and not even God will be able to fix it! Common sense is necessary in sadhana, as in everything.

Expert advice is always available and the serious sadhaka will seek it. Those who are meant to proceed on the path of sadhana will always find the proper way. However, remember that without practising preparatory sadhanas such as japa, asana, pranayama, dharana, naam japa, naam sankirtan, taking a sattwic diet, maintaining celibacy, self-improvement, mental balance, etc., the aspirant cannot be introduced to more advanced sadhana. Do not be in a hurry. Be patient and persevering, sincere and earnest.

Enhancing the practices

The duty of the aspirant is to practise sadhana. If one path of yoga sadhana is found to be inadequate, do not criticize it. Seek the advice of a master and he may add another type of yoga to it. This is how the barrier of the limited self has to be broken. If the speed of a rocket is insufficient, it will be unable to counteract the gravitational force and go beyond the sphere of gravity. In the same way, there is a law of gravity for this empirical self. People are not able to go beyond time, space and object. Although there is the ability to transcend the body and mind to some extent, one goes up and then falls back down. There must be the patience to discover the sadhana for this transcendence. In this way one will need to enhance and deepen one's practices.

Nothing comes from outside

When life is born, the atma, consciousness, brings with it eternal memories and memories inherited from parents and grandparents. There are millions of these thoughts in molecular form, called archetypes, but there is no awareness of them. They are formless and weightless, and do not require a space. At one point in the brain there may be millions of them. Some may be recognized, but there are others which have definitely not been seen in this life.

159

When sadhana is practised, these archetypes are often come across and seen in a form. Sometimes they manifest in dreams or during drowsiness. Some archetypes are associated with the process of knowledge. Maybe my father's father's grandfather knew or liked Kalidas, or maybe my father's mother's father was an astrologer. All that they knew is stored in me and sometimes it might come out at random when I practise sadhana. Just as a company must keep its account books for many years before they can be destroyed, so the brain maintains account books in a very subtle way. They are stored just like scrolls in a time capsule. Even if one can't accept the theory of transmigration, the theory of inheritance of this molecular structure of genes cannot be ignored, because it has been proved beyond doubt.

When these experiences come in sadhana, remember that nothing is coming from outside, it is all within. Every psychic experience is a passing show and there should be no attachment to it. Forget it. Keep completely free mentally, and then deeper and more profound experiences may be had.

One method of sadhana

The sadhaka should not become confused with many aims under the garb of broadmindedness. He should have one

way and one sadhana. Have faith in one God, one guru, one mantra, one religion and one method of sadhana. Do not dissipate hither and thither. Although there may be respect for different masters and spiritual paths, when it comes to personal sadhana, one guru and one set of teachings must be followed. This continuity is a very important aspect of spiritual sadhana. It is necessary so that the mind, which is dissipated and full of rajas, does not find an excuse to escape the practice. If the guru says to

160

practise japa, continue the practice without changing it. This is the only way to progress in spiritual life.

Keep sadhana sacred and secret

Sadhana is the greatest secret of yogis wishing to attain perfection. Whatever a sadhaka gains or achieves during the period of sadhana should be a private affair. To be fruitful, sadhana must be kept secret; revealed it becomes powerless. Do not act or put on a show of being a sadhaka or a yogi. Weave a defensive wall around oneself, which will not allow others to know that one has the power and light.

In the *Shiva Samhita* it says that the practitioner should keep his practice secret, "just as a virtuous wife keeps her intimate relations between herself and her husband quiet." This develops the love between husband and wife. Similarly, if there is respect for one's own beloved, the pure atma, whatever experience and power is bestowed is one's own affair and has to be cultivated privately. This is a purely logical and scientific process. A small light burning in a room at night illuminates the whole room, but outside in the vast, open space that little light is engulfed by the night and absorbed in the darkness. The same principle applies to the power gained through sadhana. The power may enlighten the aspirant's own consciousness, but displayed and dissipated in the magnitude of the outside world, it loses strength.

Keeping sadhana under cover has a powerful psychological effect. Sadhana is like a seed, which has to be left in the soil in order to germinate. If it is dug up and its progress shown to friends and neighbours, it will die and not grow any further. In the same way, if trying to cultivate fully bloomed awareness of the atma, one will have to act properly. Sadhana involves the growth of one's own spirit and the final product has to be waited for.

Yoga sadhana not only brings a balance in the energy, but also in the duality of the mind, and between the lower nature and the higher mind, between the individual soul and the universal spirit. It involves one's self and the atma, so why bring

161

anyone else into the picture? A specific sadhana is between the aspirant and the guru. Therefore, neither the practices, nor the attainments, nor the sadhana itself can be divulged to anyone. It is the guru's decision who should be given the knowledge, and it can only be gained through experience.

If attainments are talked about and displayed, the sense of 'I' or ego becomes acute. 'I' have achieved, 'I' had this experience, or 'I' can do this. If one wants to experience cosmic consciousness, ego or *ahamkara* is the greatest barrier. If one associates with the feeling that 'I' have perfected something, one will expect to be able to perform a great feat and so will others. Sadhana will start being practised merely to meet the expectations of others.

Be aware that when sadhana is practised with intensity of heart and for evolution of consciousness, a great spiritual force begins to develop within. As such, all desires for personal gain should be given up. Be prepared to discover the divine light and power unintimated, and never believe in an unalterable destiny, or *prarabdha*. Commonsense must be used at every step of sadhana. Never use willpower except in the progress of sadhana, and do not open a shop of 'blessings'. Never allow others to know about one's sadhana and siddhis. There is no merit in trying to share spiritual experiences with another. Sadhana is a sacred act, to be held in great reverence.

Siddhis

Practising yoga sadhana changes the molecular structures in the brain and makes the mind a powerful force. The mind can know things in advance and it can influence objects and impose thoughts on others. These are known as *siddhis*, psychic manifestations, and they occur in everybody who reaches a particular stage of evolution. In some aspirants they come very late in spiritual life, while in others they come early. It all depends on how highly one has evolved in a previous incarnation.

It is said in the yogic scriptures that psychic powers must be restrained, because their mental force should be preserved

162

and conserved and only utilized for higher spiritual pursuits. An aspirant who refrains from displaying his powers becomes fully illumined. Further, if the guru helps his disciples by using his siddhis, the cause of the disciple's karma will not be eliminated, and the disciple is also liable to become lazy and inactive. Instead of using his siddhis, the guru utilizes his accumulated spiritual power to help his disciples work through their karma.

When sadhana is practised without the guidance of a guru, psychic manifestations may arise, be completely misunderstood and cause havoc. Telepathy, clairvoyance and the power to influence material objects are limited and are obstacles on the spiritual path. Different siddhis or psychic powers come to a sadhaka merely to prove that he is on the way. They are never permanent, and as the mind evolves, these powers will degenerate and the yogi will come down. How will he cope when the siddhi leaves? Instead of trying to develop psychic powers and taking the risk of wandering from the higher goal, let the guru determine what one should have. If he wants to manifest psychic powers in the aspirant, he will do it. Leave everything to him.

In spiritual life it is very important to keep the ego under control. This is the reason why many people who have the capacity to exhibit psychic powers or siddhis will not do so. Most of the great saints and siddhas who had powers rarely displayed them. Only people living very close to them knew their greatness. Many siddhas who did display their powers were persecuted, as was Jesus Christ. Therefore, for the good of everyone, yogis, saints and mahatmas say, as a warning rather than as mere advice, that sadhana and siddhis are to be kept secret. If an aspirant has any knowledge of occult powers developing, it is better to ignore them. Put them in long-term fixed deposits. One day these accomplishments will pay the richest dividend in the form of perfect knowledge, *atma jnanam*.

Precisely for this reason, it is written in the yoga shastras that these accomplishments are an *upsarga*, a disease. When the sadhaka comes out of samadhi, they are known as siddhis, but when in samadhi they are obstacles. Therefore, the normal accomplishments should be used, not the spiritual ones. Swami Sivananda said the same: "Reserve the shakti of your atma. That is your earning which will be useful later on in your spiritual journey." When doing sadhana, certain accomplishments are desired, but do not use the achievements of spiritual life for any worldly purpose. Siddhis are not the desired fruit of yoga sadhana.

Always remember that the accomplishment of sadhana is not psychic powers, but jnana, knowledge of the atma. The day God begins to be perceived, even if very slightly, know that the accomplishments of sadhana are now being used. Even if it is just a foggy idea of God, realize that the karmas accumulated during numerous past lives are now coming to one's aid. The goal of all yogic sadhana is to discover and experience the universal spirit within, and if siddhis or accomplishments are indulged in, they take one away from the ultimate experience. In fact, if practised, they become the downfall of the devotee and represent a spiritual retrogression.

The *maha siddhas*, the great masters, fall into another category of rare sadhakas. They have attained powers through the perfection of the highest sadhanas and are considered to be beyond the confines of time and eventually space. These maha siddhas have accomplished the supreme goal of yoga sadhana and have released their own personalities from the cycle of birth and death in the physical world. They are *jivanmuktas*, liberated while still in the confines of prakriti. Their will is sufficiently strong to enable them to do anything, anywhere and at any time.

A maha siddha becomes omnipresent and omnipotent because he has purified and perfected the functioning of his physical and pranic bodies through mastering hatha yoga, and has transcended the normal limitations of the mind by traversing the path of raja yoga. To one immersed in the ordinary mind, such a concept as transcendence of the barriers of time and space would appear to be impossible.

164

15

A Variety of Sadhanas

Sadhana is the way to transcend the barriers of the mind. Only during sadhana is one wholly immersed in the process of delving deep within. The mind is externalized in daily life, but as far as spiritual life is concerned one has to aim for higher experiences. The role of sadhana is to pacify the wavering mind. The mind is an outcome of the three gunas: *tamas*, lethargy, *rajas*, dynamism, and *sattwa*, purity.

Due to their interplay there is conflict with the mind, which is the main cause of all the so-called miseries and bad habits, uneasiness, anger, frustration, guilt and so on. Sadhana not only controls the mind, but also erases tamas and rajas and establishes a sattwic state of mind by means of which one can lead a happy, peaceful life.

In the higher stages of sadhana, the mind becomes free from the influence of the *samskaras*, subtle impressions, of *prakriti*, the manifest universe. Sadhana is the process of purifying the inner self. When the mind becomes pure, clarity comes. To see one's own face, it is necessary to clean the mirror first.

REMEMBERING GOD'S NAME

Remembrance of God's name, *naam smarana*, is the highest sadhana. The name of the Lord is the greatest gift one can have. The glory of the name is beyond the comprehension of the human mind. It may seem to be just a few syllables, but in reality it is not, for the intellect fails to understand the wonder and working power of the name, which removes *avidya*, gross ignorance.

This name is a mantra. Repetition of a mantra is called *japa*. Chanting the mantra verbally or mentally harmonizes the whole mind. Constant repetition alters the consciousness. The aspirant is less influenced by the ups and downs of the tumultuous world and becomes more aware. The whole mind becomes concentrated and powerful. Continual remembrance will break down the ego and identification with the body and mind, and lead to knowledge and fulfilment.

According to all the revelations, the best sadhana for future generations and the coming age is repetition of God's name. This has been the experience of saints throughout the centuries. Swami Sivananda used to say that the highest sadhana is repeating God's name. It is said in the Bible, Koran and other scriptures that people must remember and sing God's name with devotion. This practice will bring good results to the practitioner and to others as well. It will be the greatest yoga, the yoga for everyone.

There has always been yoga for the few, the privileged, yoga teachers and acharyas, but not everybody can do higher practices. It has been said that people in the coming age will become restless, greedy, passionate and unable to find peace, but if they practise repeating the Lord's name, they will find peace. It is not necessary to renounce one's home for the sake of sadhana, but an unshakeable faith and love for the Lord will have to be awakened in the heart. Remember God throughout the day. It is not necessary to sit in one place to repeat His name. Repeat the name in any way, anywhere and whenever one likes, but do it with *bhava*, intense awareness. Try to keep the mind in tune with the name and firmly anchored to it.

Between completing one task and beginning another, leisure time can always be found. The mantra can be repeated during such periods. Let mental remembrance of God and the mantra evolve as natural aspects of one's being, so that even during sleep the mantra continues to be repeated. Do not forget the mantra even for a second. Ultimately, in the higher stages of sadhana, the whole of life must be dedicated to His awareness. There is no holiday from, or reserved hours, for sadhana. It should be regular, constant and unceasing. Avoid reflecting on the past or anticipating the future, but try to be in the immediate present.

Beware that the thoughts do not roam aimlessly when lying down to sleep. Every minute is precious for a yogi. Every second is precious for a real sadhu. Whenever there is time, merge in japa, introvert the mind, peep within and experience joy. If continual remembrance is not possible, then at least remembering the name with devotion in the morning on waking and when sleeping at night will saturate the whole mind with positive thoughts and vibrations.

The path of spiritual sadhana is long and arduous. If it were easier, then everyone would attain enlightenment without effort. People have been making effort after effort to seek God in their minds. However, at the last moment the Lord's name does not come. The mental conditioning is such that at the last moment one says, "Call my daughter-in-law; call my son." One is unable to utter anything else.

Bhakti yoga sadhana

Ceaseless remembrance is a powerful practice for expanding awareness, but it is not easy without devotion. There has to be a natural attraction for the sweetness of the name of one's deity, just as bees are automatically attracted to the nectar in a flower. Love, constant awareness and devotion intensifies this remembrance. Love means there will be unceasing thirst, unforgettable remembrance and unswerving aspiration to unite with one's *ishta* or chosen deity. This practice should not be done occasionally during prayers, but twenty-four hours a day. Remember each and every moment, with every heartbeat, with every breath and with every action. This is the sadhana of bhakti yoga.

With this intensity, aspiration and bhakti, the remembrance will become natural and spontaneous. One will want to remember, for the name is associated with *prem*, intense love. It is the focal point of all the emotions and feelings. Remember the name as the bhakta or devotee remembers his beloved, as the miser greedy for riches remembers wealth

and the murderer remembers the police due to fear. There is no effort, it is involuntary; they have no choice but to remember. A bhakta must remember God, his guru and mantra or whatever with the same intensity.

Try to hear and feel divinity everywhere. Whenever the mind feels inclined to meditate, close the eyes, feel the presence of the divine power and realize the mystic vibrations everywhere. Shut out the experience of sense consciousness, and in the vacuum so created try to visualize God. Take this divine anaesthesia. Pay no attention to the mind; do not fight with it. In this way, when fully saturated with the divine inflow, bring the form of the ishta into the vacuum. This is the way to perfect higher sadhana.

Every act must become worship. It is not necessary to read countless numbers of scriptures, or practise one thousand and one yogic practices in sadhana. The whole being has to be submerged in continuous repetition of the mantra. There has to be complete surrender. Divinity has to be felt everywhere. Try to see divinity in every part of the world without exception. Try to feel this in the heart. This is the way to union with the inner world of knowledge.

In this way, His remembrance must permeate the whole being twenty-four hours a day. The divine will then descends and one realizes that every pleasure is His, every breath is His miracle, every day is His glory – and one is His manifestation. There comes a moment when the soul awakens – then the essential unity between the sentient and the insentient is realized.

There are many cases of great bhaktas who were unable to stop remembering even when they were dying It is said that when Mahatma Gandhi was assassinated he said only one thing, "Ram, Ram, Ram." His ceaseless remembrance continued even when he was dying.

Many of the great poets have illustrated this continual remembrance. For them the supreme is a helper, a dearest and nearest friend, nearer than the breath, nearer than their own mind. This is beautifully expressed by Lord Tennyson:

Speak to Him, for He hears
And spirit to spirit can speak.
Nearer is He than breathing,
Closer than hands and feet.

When one has this intensity of feeling, how is it possible not to remember? And this is the express train to expanded awareness. The great bhakta Ramdas said, "The quickest and easiest way to the Supreme is to remember Him always by repeating His sweet and powerful name." Ramdas practised *mantra upasana*, worship through mantra. This sadhana included continuous mental and verbal chanting of a mantra, visualization of the form of guru in the heart centre and identifying every object on which the mind dwells with divinity. Whatever Ramdas thought of became the form of the Supreme.

It is said that when the name of the Supreme is chanted unceasingly, He Himself will chase one. Kabir sang,

I have regained my pristine condition,
It is indescribable.
My mind has become crystal clear
like the water of the Ganges.
God himself keeps following me
and calling, 'O Kabir'.

Only a person who has merged in the exalted state of samadhi could say this. His main sadhana was continual remembrance, but it seems that when he sang this song, he had left all sadhanas behind. His path of devotion with continual remembrance had launched him into the transcendental realms.

KIRTAN – SADHANA FOR KALI YUGA

When groups of four or more people join together in a group and sing the name of God, it is called kirtan or *naam sankirtan*. Kirtan is the main sadhana of Kali yuga, the present age. Tulsidas, Chaitanya Mahaprabhu and other saints and mahatmas used to say that in Kali yuga all the paths to reach God are very difficult. The only simple path is kirtan; it is the only sadhana that can be done with relaxation and without difficulty.

This age is very complex, full of tensions and preoccupations. People are never free; they have to work to support the family, so there is not a lot of time. Even if there is time, it is extremely difficult to concentrate the mind. Everybody has a restless mind; it cannot remain at one point and so it is very difficult to practise many sadhanas. Concentration of mind is very difficult in this age. Even without family problems, no matter how good, virtuous, honest, calm and quiet a person may be, the mind still cannot be concentrated.

Different yugas have had different methods of sadhana such as yajna, tapasya, tyaga, yoga and so on, but in Kali yuga, these methods are not very common and most people are not capable of performing them, as the mind becomes lost. *Tyaga*, renunciation, or *tapasya*, austerity, make people ill. *Yajna*, fire sacrifice, is time consuming so there would be no time left for a job or business, and it also costs a lot of money. Asana, pranayama, neti and dhauti may be practised for the body, but all the other sadhanas for God realization, for leading a divine life, have become redundant because they are too difficult. Therefore, kirtan is the simplest, easiest and surest sadhana, involving the least risk and expense.

There are different feelings and attitudes towards God. *Kirtan* is singing about God's *mahima* or greatness, His attributes, His compassion, His grace, His ability to take away sorrow. Singing the name of God with adoration is *bhajan*. Singing the praises of the Lord is *stuti*. *Naam smarana* means remembering the name of God. Asking the Lord for something through song or praying to God to be kind, to be merciful, to bring peace of mind is called *prarthana*.

Sing His name repeatedly in harmony, with a lot of people or with family members, for one hour or longer. Play a guitar, a mridanga or a harmonium, and just keep on singing. When ten, twenty, thirty or more people sing kirtan together, a combined powerful energy is generated. The house where kirtan is sung is purified because kirtan removes all the bad spirits, so that people will remain in a positive mental state. All the rubbish disappears, because the name of God has the ability to destroy negative energy. When the light of the sun appears, the darkness disappears. The name of God is like light, enlightening and purifying wherever it exists.

For those who are crooked, who have tensions at home, sorrow, misfortune or health problems, it is useless to even talk about concentration. Even with complete harmony in the family, the mind is not able to concentrate. In Kali yuga, concentration of mind is only possible for a few people; it cannot be done by everybody. However, it is still possible to sing God's name all together and become immersed in the vibrations for an hour or so.

PRAYER – A POWERFUL SADHANA

When there is the urge to do sadhana, pray to God. Ask Him, "What should I do?" and He will give the inspiration. Wherever one is, He is there. Pray to Him and He will show the way. God can show the way to anybody. Whoever seeks the way with a true heart and labours for it will be shown the true way by the Lord. Prayer is a powerful way to give expression to the suppressed emotions and thought forms of the mind. During prayer, the Lord is a symbol which is imagined or visualized and to which one offers all the expressions of the heart. This process purifies and relaxes the mind, which is the immediate relevance of prayer to everyday life. Prayer has a deeper significance in regard to spiritual enlightenment, however, where the aspirant is communicating with the inner self.

Prayer presupposes an attentive mind towards the object of prayer. Japa is meant to awaken spiritual power, while prayer directs that power to a particular and desired end. Hence, prayer can be done at the end of japa, concentration and meditation. Maha mantra and Mahamrityunjaya and other mantras can form the basis of the prayer at the end of

172

sadhana. Remember, however, that the guru mantra is only for repetition, and while repeating it, no one else but the form should be in one's mind. If the aspirant sticks to the guru mantra, that will give all that is prayed for.

Feel as if He is standing there; kneel before Him and tell Him all the troubles, accomplishments, emotions and worries. Let it take one, two or even three hours. It will be remove a lot of the mental burden from one's shoulders. Prayer is the purgative which removes the fermented waste from the system. It means that nothing should be hidden from Him. Go to Him naked and empty. Though the beloved Lord knows everything, still He has to be told in order to remove the dirt from the mind. Prayer is the most effective medicine, and it will not cost anything.

Remember that prayer is effective only if the meaning is understood. Either follow the Sanskrit directly, or pray in the language that is understood well. It is necessary for a sadhaka to know what he is praying for. If a prayer is made for the welfare, wellbeing and prosperity of one's family or others, it immediately becomes efficacious. Such prayers purify the mind, and at the same time make the thought force more potent.

Pray in all love, humility and confidence. The prayer mixed with emotion and feeling is at once heard and fulfilled. Do not simply utter Sanskrit verses which are not understood. Pray to

Him like a child. Remember any event of life when the prayer was heard and fulfilled, and recollect that state of mind. Pray with perfect faith that He will listen to the prayer and fulfil it. Never pray for trifles. Pray to Him for the strength to face life. Pray for *viveka*, discrimination, *vairagya*, dispassion, love and service. Pray for purity of mind, for meditation and continence. Pray to Him to come face to face and reveal His knowledge. Have faith that He is all-merciful and a kind Father, and that He will give all one asks for. Pray to Him for quick spiritual evolution with love, faith and *bhava*, intense emotion.

THE FOUR MAJOR YOGAS

Karma yoga, bhakti yoga, raja yoga and jnana yoga are the four main yogas, and they are designed to suit different temperaments. Karma yoga is suitable for people who are dynamic, bhakti yoga for those who are emotional, raja yoga is more suitable for psychic people, and jnana yoga for those are rational by temperament. However, a combination of these has to be practised because human beings are a combination of all the qualities. One quality may predominate, but the other qualities will also be present. Therefore, it is better to have a synthesis of all the yoga practices. The aspirant needs to specialize in the yoga that is most appropriate, but also devote some time to the other practices.

Karma yoga, the yoga of selfless action, or action without attachment, is best for those who want to work and express themselves through work. Bhakti yoga suits those who have a surplus of emotion, which needs to be properly channelled so that it does not create problems in the mind. Bhakti can be practised by offering the surplus love to guru, to God, to humanity, to everybody.

In raja yoga, one tries to discover the deeper forms of mental experience not accessible through the external senses. Ultimately this inner realm leads to expansion of consciousness. When consciousness expands and becomes one with totality, it is called *samadhi*. Jnana yoga is a sadhana of dis-

174

covering one's inner being by a process of deep thinking, rationalization and contemplation. Through introspection, the higher truth is heard and by reflecting on that, one can have direct cognition of the wider truth.

It is said in jnana yoga and in Vedanta that one hears the truth from the guru, contemplates that truth and then realizes that truth. This is the basic philosophy of jnana yoga. If the supreme experience could be achieved by reflection, contemplation or self-introspection alone, then why is it necessary to practise all these yogas? Just sit down and ask, "Who am I? I am not this body, I am not this mind, I am not these senses." Go on doing this and a point will come when the question arises, "Do I have the intensity of awareness to actually do it? Am I able to think about knowledge of the self without any hindrance or interruption?"

If an unbroken flow of self-awareness can be maintained, then one belongs on the path of jnana yoga. Just sit down and contemplate whatever has been heard from the guru and maintain that awareness in an unbroken flow, without letting any other thought intrude or letting the external awareness be a disturbance.

To practise jnana yoga, however, there must be sufficient control over the influences of the mind. In order to develop control over the mind, raja yoga must be practised. Without concentration, the mind cannot be controlled, and to develop concentration bhakti yoga has to be practised. The mind must be pure to achieve concentration, not soiled like an upset stomach, passing wind or belching all the time. The mind can be cleaned by practising karma yoga.

This is the chronological order. Practise karma yoga and clean the mind; then practise bhakti yoga and achieve concentration; then practise raja yoga and develop control over the mind, and finally practise jnana yoga and contemplate the truth. These are the graded steps towards jnana yoga. Jnana yoga alone cannot give the ultimate experience without first preparing the body and mind, without developing mental control, without concentration and so on.

175

GENERAL YOGA SADHANA

To practise yoga sadhana, one must undergo some self-imposed discipline in order to condition the body, mind, intellect and emotions and remove physical and mental faults. In general, anyone who wants to reap the benefits of yoga sadhana should practise asanas for ten minutes, pranayama for three to five minutes and concentration for ten minutes. Only half an hour daily needs to be dedicated to the practices of yoga. If concentration is practised regularly and sincerely with correct understanding, ten minutes daily is enough. Results have even been noticed in five minutes. Anyone who subjects themselves to seven or eight hours of yoga is overdoing it. Even sannyasins who have renounced the world are not allowed to practise for such extended periods of time.

Asana

Some asanas suit practically everybody. Children, young people, and older people who are used to exercise should practise surya namaskara every day. It is a dynamic exercise with beneficial and vitalizing effects on all parts of the body and mind. The second asana is vajrasana. It is a very relaxing position, both physically and mentally and it also stimulates the digestive processes, especially if assumed for a few minutes after meals. The third asana, shashankasana, is especially recommended for people with stiff backs or digestive disorders such as constipation and indigestion. It is one of the best asanas for invigorating the whole brain.

The fourth asana, ardha matsyendrasana, the spinal twist pose, should be included to ensure that the spinal column is given a good twist in both directions. It will supplement the forward and backward bending movements of the other asanas. As well as manipulating the spinal cord it also benefits the abdominal organs and the muscles and nerves of the back. The fifth asana is paschimottanasana. Hold it for ten to thirty seconds at first and then release the posture. Repeat and then lie down in shavasana, the corpse pose, and do not move the body for one or two minutes.

Most people can practise these basic asanas. Other practices are necessary for older people, invalids, overweight people, or anyone who cannot manage the more advanced asanas. Such people should practise the pawanmuktasana series, which are designed to remove gastric and rheumatic problems. *Pawan* means wind, acid or gas, and *mukta* means release or free. The pawanmuktasana exercises are very simple movements which make the whole body supple and can be practised by people of eighty or ninety.

Pranayama

Pranayama practice need only take five minutes. There are two important techniques. One is nadi shodhana pranayama, alternate nostril breathing. Another easier pranayama is ujjayi, which is done by contracting the epiglottis. It is the same

177

type of breathing done in deep sleep, like mild snoring. In the beginning, choose one of these practices and make it part of the regular sadhana.

Concentration

The third set of practices is to concentrate the mind. Concentration bestows keen insight and paves the way for intuitional flashes of discovery. The method of concentrating the mind should be based on the personality. For example, if the mind is restless or it will not allow one to sit still for a short time, then mantra and antar mouna should be practised. Do not suppress or discard the thoughts. Witness the whole thought process without creating any barrier, but at the same time go on repeating the mantra.

People with a rajasic temperament are always restless and cannot still the mind even for a second. Sometimes when they practise Om chanting, for the whole five minutes their mind will be thinking about horrible things from the past, whereas on other days it will be quiet. Nevertheless, they should continue to practise and try to develop the ability to remain as a witness of the thoughts.

People with a sattwic temperament have fewer problems with the mind and rarely experience restlessness. They should practise concentration at the mid-eyebrow centre, trying to visualize a symbol of their choice, such as a yantra, mandala or their ishta devata. People who are tamasic in nature start dozing or dreaming whenever they sit for concentration. They should not try to withdraw the mind because the moment they close their eyes to practise japa, they start to see visions and many other things. Loud mantra chanting or kirtan is most suitable for them.

The concentration practice must be chosen according to one's state of evolution. Whenever sadhana is practised, begin and end by chanting Om aloud. Learn these practices from an experienced teacher to ensure that there are no harmful side effects.

178

One practice is enough

For a beginner, yoga means just ten to fifteen minutes practice daily, not forty-five minutes or one hour. This is based on objective research. One single asana, shashankasana or sarvangasana, is enough. People suffering from heart disease are taught just one practice, not a complicated sadhana of twenty asanas, fifteen pranayamas, thirteen mudras, fourteen kriyas and so on. Each asana and pranayama is a complete unit capable of hitting the disease so hard that a few minutes practice is enough.

Just as one does not increase the amount of food one eats, it is also not necessary to increase the amount of practice. Five rounds means five rounds only. Just as two meals a day gives enough energy for all one's activities, in the same way, practising yoga for a short time in the morning and evening will keep a person balanced and consistent throughout the day. Too much yoga too quickly means increasing the will beyond its capacity. Trying too hard will only lead to feeling exhausted, frustrated and leaving the sadhana before anything concrete has been received from it. Sadhana is not a game of table tennis or cards.

Today, even if people want to devote their whole life to yoga and spiritual achievements, they are not able to do so. They cannot even spare ten minutes for asanas and pranayama. Therefore, people with spiritual aspirations should start with the minimum amount of time. Instead of trying to devote two or three hours every day, which will gradually be reduced to nil anyway, it is preferable to first start with ten minutes, so that in the course of time all the energies and interests are crystallized. The time of practice will then increase automatically according to necessity, capacity and motivation.

Ten minutes every day

In 1943 my guru, Swami Sivananda, gave me a mantra and told me to practise five malas every day. At that early stage I was not aware of the importance of malas and mantras, but

179

I began and the practice took no longer than three minutes. Meanwhile I started reading books on different philosophies and I began to think that God did not exist and that everything in this life was false. Then I started to wonder about the mantra, whether it was also only humbug and I wanted to renounce it in favour of atheism. These were five very critical years when my mind was always at boiling point. I had to fight between my intellectualism, emotions, passions, spirit, guru, god, culture and tradition.

However, with my guru's guidance I continued to practise five malas regularly every day and during this period the most important link in my life was formed in those three minutes. Had I renounced my link with the mantra, I would never have achieved what I have achieved. These five malas saved me so that today I stand firmly as a swami, holding the torch of a spiritual culture.

Practise yoga sadhana for ten minutes during the day. What can one lose in this short time? During the practice, forget money, relationships, work and the telephone. Ten minutes every day makes three hundred minutes every month, 3,600 minutes every year. This ten minutes a day is the premium one pays for spiritual happiness.

SHORT SADHANA FOR EMOTIONAL TENSION

Life and death, success and failure, love and hatred all cause emotional tension, and everyone experiences them day in and day out throughout life. Therefore, one should learn how to eliminate these tensions. Although yoga has many excellent techniques to offer, there is one short, effective sadhana.

First practise the surya namaskara series. Afterwards sit quietly, close the eyes and concentrate on the normal and natural breath for as long as possible. That is the practice with which meditation begins. Just close the eyes and concentrate on the breath flowing through the nostrils. After a short time the body and mind will become calm and quiet. Start with five minutes and then increase to fifteen minutes.

180

Then, start repeating a mantra. If any thought comes to the mind, do not try to block it. Just see what it is and continue repeating the mantra. Do not be disturbed by any kind of thought or feeling. Whether there is a vicious thought or a pleasant thought, do not interfere with the thought process. Bad memories should come, impure thoughts must arise and the purging must be complete. After that, a complete novice will feel totally relaxed as though he has come out of a mental crisis. This short sadhana can remove emotional tension.

When the thoughts are suppressed, the mental energy becomes blocked, but when the thoughts are allowed free movement, the mind becomes relaxed. This practice is known as *antar mouna*, inner silence. In order to silence the mind it is not necessary to suppress and punish it. When the stomach is upset, it is allowed to purge itself. At first, purging can cause discomfort, and going to the toilet frequently can be very tiring, but ultimately it will relax the whole stomach. It is the same with the mind.

The mind is overloaded with various kinds of thoughts. Where there are complexes and conflicts, there is schizophrenia. There are worries, anxieties and passions, love and hatred, fear and insecurity, and many others. Some are known and some are not, but all these thoughts are lying hidden in the mind. Sometimes they express themselves during dreams or sickness, but it is far better if these grosser elements are cleansed from the mind through the process of meditation.

A person must be able to master the different realms of life. If this can be understood, then one is ready for the formula. Only a few asanas and pranayamas need be practised every day and ten or fifteen minutes dedicated to mantra and meditation.

CHILDREN AND SPIRITUAL SADHANA

In India, during the time of the Vedas, there was a tradition that every child at the age of seven or eight was taught three practices: surya namaskara, pranayama and Gayatri mantra. Children were then sent to the gurukul for further education for a period of twelve years, where they were taught all the sciences by the guru. Nowadays this initiation is merely a ritual in India, and its practical value is not really understood. However, over the last decades I have spoken on this topic in schools and colleges everywhere and children have become aware of the reasons why they should practise yoga in their early years.

The family home should become like an ashram where children can play, read and talk to their parents as if they were friends. Do children speak the truth to their parents? Do their parents allow them to speak the truth? If parents want their children to be truthful, they must be very relaxed with them. Ethics, morality, purity and religion are the breeding grounds of total hypocrisy, sad incidents and accidents in history. Do not try to breed a generation of hypocrites, but a generation which can speak the truth, for whom there is nothing else except truth. Truth means 'as it is'.

Children should not be products of religion, ethics and morality, but products of love and understanding and the deep-rooted intimate relationship between mother, father and children. The family must become an ashram, a community of friends, where parents and children live together. They have different roles within the family structure such as husband and wife, brother and sister, parents and children, but all are members of the same family.

Gifted children

From time to time there have been children gifted with spiritual awareness to whom the general theory of teaching yoga to children does not apply. Gifted children should be taught more about spiritual life, inner awareness and the deep-rooted psychic and spiritual forces within, so that in times to come they can develop into geniuses.

It is said that when Adi Shankaracharya was eight years old, he developed absolute awareness. He then thought of becoming a sannyasin, but his widowed mother would not allow him. Somehow he secured her permission and went in search of a guru. When he found his guru, he stayed with him for eight years and learned the ancient wisdom, both theory and practice. At the age of sixteen, he set out from his guru's ashram and travelled the length and breadth of India, preaching unqualified monism, *adwaita vedanta*, not only the doctrine of one God, but the doctrine of oneness, which means everything is just one. At that age, he was able to convince the intellectuals and the masses, as well as his opponents. At the age of thirty-two he died. Such people are called gifted children.

When Christ was a child, he was supposed to have lived for some time in an Essene monastery. The monks there found him extraordinary and perhaps they could not cope with his eagerness, intuition, and wisdom. So, when he was thirteen, he was sent to India, where he lived for twelve years in various parts of the country, including Kashmir, Nepal, Jagannath Puri and the famous Nalanda University, only a hundred miles south of Munger. He met a lot of people who had both theoretical and practical knowledge. There are many such stories of inspired and gifted children.

Expose children to spiritual activities

If children are exposed to a spiritual environment, they can develop the inner seed of spiritual awareness. Every child is pure, untainted and innocent. Children have awareness of their inner self. Adults do not have that awareness. Books tell people that they have a self, atma, soul, spirit, and they accept it, but they do not really experience it. All the emotions, fears, love, agony and depression, sleep, hunger and pain are experienced, but the self is not experienced.

Gradually as the worldly maya enveloped the child in the form of desires and ambitions, the idea of the self was completely lost. It is said in the Bible, "Be like a child", which means be thoughtless, desireless and free. Frustration or depression, death or birth, profit or loss, victory or conquest is all a drama, a game; it is not reality. With a free mind that childlike awareness can be maintained all the time.

Therefore, expose children to spiritual and yogic activities. Those who are not spiritually evolved should be given yoga, pranayama, mantra, surya namaskara, etc. for their spiritual growth. Those who have come with spiritual potential from their previous life will be known at once and must be given the opportunity to find their own path. They will discover a way for themselves and they will also discover the sadhana which they have to do for their spiritual illumination.

SADHANA FOR BUSINESS PEOPLE

People involved in the business world must find some time for yoga sadhana, ten minutes to half an hour either in the morning or evening, as convenient. Let them learn the practices of yoga in a way that is acceptable and according to their needs, because they have to remain occupied in their business. A short sadhana can be practised at home to remove many

184

problems. If staff, executives and administrators devote some of their time to yoga sadhana, even if they do not develop efficiency, that can go a long way towards preventing stress, strain, nervous breakdown, hypertension and so forth. In this manner they will discover that the mind and body are important for each other. The mind is important, but the body carries it. A short daily yoga sadhana can bring about a great change in the mind.

SADHANA FOR THE ELDERLY

If yoga is taken up at an advanced age, there will certainly be restrictions. One does not start with padmasana or dhanurasana, but with pawanmuktasana and other light practices. Elderly people usually have enormous experience of life and awareness, but they are without a centre where everything can be aligned and streamlined. Therefore, under proper guidance they can practise mantra and a few hatha yoga exercises, and then yoga nidra can be added.

Another important form of yoga for elderly people is kundalini yoga. They should practise sending their awareness up and down the spine from mooladhara chakra at the base to ajna chakra at the top, maintaining a constant stream of consciousness. This can be practised while lying on the back or while sitting in a chair. Gradually, this practice will awaken the responses in the channels that flow within the framework of the spine and connect these two important chakras.

It is much more difficult to practise sadhana when one becomes old and infirm and unable to stretch the limbs and lie down. If sadhana is reserved for old age, it can never be practised into the higher stages. Old age is the time for rest. Yoga can be practised at any time, but youth provides the best opportunity to begin sadhana. In youth, sadhana enhances the pleasure of living.

MOUNA SADHANA

Mouna is a powerful practice to energize the system and develop inner sensitivity. When a transistor is played for twenty-four hours, the battery will go flat, but if it is switched off, the battery will last longer. That is the importance of *mouna*, or silence. The human battery is pranic energy, and it is used up quickly in speaking, listening, thinking, walking, worrying and passions. The pranic energy spent on all these activities should be conserved. Staying silent for some time will conserve mental energy. Conservation of prana is the solution to the personal energy crisis.

Talk only when necessary. Mouna should be observed in the form of sadhana and *swadhyaya*, self-analysis. In spiritual sadhana useless talking will retard progress. Make it a point to talk to the point and simplify answers. The aim is 'essential talking', which will not only minimize verbal commitments, but help in meditation as well. Observe mouna on Sundays as well as on other holidays, when it is appropriate to the situation.

The practice of mouna has its special merits and karma yoga has its own merits too. Practising silence for a day or

186

two will enhance one's meditation practice because the mind becomes more tranquil, but if silence is practised for a few months or years, then the samskaras are purged at a greater speed than they would through the practice of karma yoga.

By means of karma yoga self-awareness can be developed, and as awareness increases many hidden things are gradually revealed. However, when mouna is practised during karma yoga, awareness develops at a faster speed and karmas are purged at a greater pace. Therefore, a synthesis between karma yoga and mouna should be developed, so that the karmas can be expelled in a systematic way. Then the sadhana becomes more successful.

SADHANA AT THE TIME OF DEATH

Always pray, "Oh Lord, do me this one favour. When the breath stops, let my last word be your name."

O Krishna, O Yadava, O Friend,
At the time of death, please come before me
Playing on the flute and delighting my mind.
I wish to sing Your names while dying,
Govinda, Damodara and Madhava.

O devotee, do you think this is your mind?
What did you bring when you came?
And what will you take when you depart?
Only these names will always remain with you,
Govinda, Damodara and Madhava.

The breath has to stop sometime. When a person dies, the breath stops either while inhaling or while exhaling. The last breath should be awareness of the mantra. It does not matter where one dies. The important thing is awareness at the last breath.

WHATEVER ONE DOES BECOMES SADHANA

Whatever one does or wants to do can become a sadhana provided it is offered to God. The feeling that 'I am the doer' must not be there. Some people work as doctors, some as lawyers, some as priests, some do business. Whatever the work, there must be a feeling of dedication.

Action performed not for oneself but for others is selfless action. In *grihastha ashrama*, householder life, there is more possibility for selfless action, since everything a householder produces and whatever actions he performs are not done merely for himself. Everything is done for the family, for relatives, for dependents and for the society he lives in. Everyone owes a large debt to society. If society becomes unstable, one will not be able to run to a shop or buy or sell goods or go to the bank.

To repay this debt to society, one has to put aside part of one's earnings. It is necessary for the well-off sectors to support and uplift the weaker sectors of society who are in need. If that sector is neglected, people will not be able to live and trade in security. Remember that whatever is produced or earned should be distributed judiciously among oneself, one's children and dependents, as well as for education, medical care, distributing food and feeding the poor. Such a distribution of wealth must be carried out. This is also considered a sadhana.

In this way, everyone must work without any desire for the fruits of their actions. When that level of consciousness is developed, an unbelievable awakening will take place within, which can be called *chetana*, consciousness, or *atman*, soul. This means that one's individual boundaries must not be narrow and small. 'This is mine, that is yours' are the thoughts of narrow-minded people. For one with a big heart, the whole of creation is one family. It is also said in the *Mahabharata* that for the generous hearted, the whole world is a family.

One has to discharge one's duties side by side with one's spiritual sadhana. In the same way it should always be remembered that not only this body but one's family, relatives and property are also His gifts. Not for a moment should it be forgotten that He alone looks after all one's needs. This attitude will not only remove worries and fears, but also bestow immense spiritual stamina.

SPIRITUAL DIARY

A spiritual diary should tell a saga of spiritual effort and progress. A diary should not be written for artistic style or to display one's experiences for publication. It should be written from inner necessity and include anything concerning sadhana. Reading the diary will help in meditation.

The spiritual diary must include inspiring ideas. Here are some samples: "Even as butter is hidden in milk, likewise light and power are hidden within this body. I am light and power. I am not this body, not this mind, not these senses."

"Even when I am profoundly asleep, the experience of bliss and existence remains intact. This proves that in the absence of all sense activities, the light and power remain unaffected."

"I am all-powerful. I am that infinite light which permeates everywhere. Sins do not contaminate me. Pain does not touch me. Injuries do not hurt me. A sword cannot kill me. Water cannot drench me. Fire cannot burn me. I am an unchangeable and permanent wall upon which the changing scenes of the world come and go. I am one as well as many. I work through infinite hands. I eat through infinite mouths. I look out through infinite eyes. I am the life and protector of the infinite universe. I give light to the sun. I love all, for 'all' are nothing but 'my own self'."

A spiritual diary is an immense aid in sadhana, self-analysis and spiritual progress. It is a method of correcting habits, remodelling behaviour and cultivating virtues. As a method of self-evaluation, a spiritual diary can include the following questions.

What was the time of rising in the morning? Note the time of rising and remember that the purpose is not to compel one to rise earlier by launching a fight against the habits, but to refashion the underground structure of the habit itself.

How many hours were spent sleeping? People become confused because they are unable to decide the minimum and maximum hours of sleep required. People need as much sleep as is required for proper decarbonization of the system, which may differ from individual to individual. The average requirement is six hours for intellectuals, eight hours for manual labourers and four hours for sadhakas. One who has attained samadhi does not need sleep at all. Those who sleep in excess may have accumulated toxins in the system, or psychological suppressions or deeply engrained tensions, maybe due to failure in their career. A normal person does not oversleep. The hours of sleep can be minimized by eating a sattwic diet, and practising asanas and meditation.

How long were asanas and pranayama practised? Practise asanas for fifteen minutes daily. Select a few asanas or have them selected by the guru. The duration of pranayama should be noted, which is from five to fifteen minutes.

How much time was spent in pooja, prayer or meditation? Some aspirants practise meditation, some *naam smarana*, remembrance of God's name, and others say prayers. Note down this item according to the daily practice. If all three are being practised, write them down separately.

How many malas of japa were performed? This is an important item. Make a resolve to do a certain number of malas daily. Over-enthusiasm is not good. Japa should be done with the guru mantra as given during mantra initiation; not just taken from a hatha yoga teacher or a book as many aspirants do.

The aspirant will have to note down all the difficulties and complexes faced and preserve such notes in the sadhana room. Whenever there is restlessness or depression, go to the sadhana room, meditate for a while and look at the positive resolves. Note these resolves in the diary. This will help to achieve peace of mind. Failing to act according to one's resolve means lack of willpower.

Which good quality is being cultivated? First of all resolve to cultivate one good quality, but it should not be a difficult one. For instance, resolve to speak less and avoid irrelevant, useless, sensational and futile talk. Month by month, choose one yama and niyama and go on cultivating good virtues in this manner.

How many times did anger arise, and which method of self-management or self-discipline was practised? The form of discipline for this act of indiscrimination and foolishness must be decided upon; for example, resolving not to speak harsh words.

How many hours of selfless service were performed and what was learnt? Selfless service purifies the soul. Due to selfishness, the entire personality is lost in darkness. If selfless service is practised, life will grow in happiness and the mind will become strong and powerful.

These are a few ideas for keeping a spiritual diary. Other entries may include inspiring ideas, and the inspiration ob-

191

tained from swadhyaya and from satsang. Make a new diary every month and add new items to it. After some time, by the grace of God, the aspirant will become established in the daily practice of sadhana and side by side live a divine life.

Glossary

Abhyasa – constant and steady practice without any interruption; to remain established in the effort of sadhana

Adi Shankaracharya – a celebrated teacher of Adwaita Vedanta who wrote commentaries on the major Upanishads, the Bhagavad Gita and Brahma Sutras; founder of the Dashnami tradition of sannyasa

Adwaita Vedanta – philosophy of unqualified monism, the doctrine of one God, and also the doctrine of oneness which means everything is just one

Agama – esoteric tradition of tantra suitable for Kali yuga, the present age

Ahamkara – egoism or self-conceit; 'I am-ness', self-consciousness; the principle responsible for the limitations, division and variety in the manifest world; the rajasic state of consciousness limiting awareness of existence

Ajapa japa – continuous, spontaneous repetition of mantra; meditation practice in which mantra is coordinated with breath

Ajna chakra – the third eye, the command or monitoring psychic/pranic centre, also known as the guru chakra

Akhanda – unbroken, ongoing

Ananda – pleasure, happiness; pure unalloyed bliss; state of consciousness

Antahkarana – inner organ, instrument or tool of consciousness; mind

Antar mouna – inner silence; meditative technique belonging to the fifth step of raja yoga (pratyahara), consisting of six stages

Antaranga mukha vritti – internal awareness

Anugraha – divine grace

Anushthana – a resolve to perform mantra sadhana with absolute discipline for a requisite period of time

193

Asamprajnata samadhi – state of identification of the individual consciousness with the universal state of existence and consciousness

Asana – in raja yoga, a physical posture in which one is at ease and in harmony with oneself; posture for meditation or for health; in hatha yoga, a specific body posture to balance and channel energy (prana), open the chakras and remove energy blocks

Atma – the self beyond mind and body; supreme consciousness, spirit, soul

Atma chintan – introspection; reflection on the self or the atman

Atma jnana – direct knowledge of the self

Atma vichara – enquiry into the nature of the self

Avadhoota – one who is free from all worldly attachments or mental illusions; sixth order of sannyasa; the highest state of asceticism or tapas

Avidya – ignorance; lack of conscious awareness; mistaking the non-eternal for the eternal

Bahiranga mukha vritti – external awareness

Bandha – psycho-muscular energy locks; postural contraction of the body

Bhagavad Gita – 'divine song', Lord Krishna's discourse to Arjuna delivered on the battlefield of Kurukshetra during the great Mahabharata war

Bhakta – devotee

Bhakti – complete devotion to the higher reality of life; love for all beings; channelling of emotion to a higher force

Bhakti yoga – yoga of devotion, channelling emotional energy to a higher reality of life; a systematic path with nine steps or stages expanding, strengthening and purifying the emotions

Bhava – feeling; love; inclination or disposition of mind

Bhoga – experience and craving for pleasure

Brahmacharya – conduct suitable for proceeding to the highest state of existence, especially continence or absolute control of sensual impulses

Brahmamuhurta – the two hours around sunrise (in India between 4 am and 6 am) most auspicious for spiritual sadhana

Brahma vidya – knowledge of Brahman (the supreme existence)

Chetana – unmanifest aspect of consciousness and energy

Chidakasha – the space or sphere within, where the capacity of sense perception is internalized to observe the process and reactions of individual awareness; the inner space visualized in meditation behind the closed eyes or in the region of ajna chakra; the state of pure, unbounded consciousness

Chitta – individual consciousness, including the subconscious and unconscious layers of mind; storehouse of memory or samskaras

Dama – control of the outer senses; self-command through self-restraint and curbing the passions

Darshan – a glimpse, seeing, observing; sight, vision; knowing, understanding

Deva – luminous being; a god or divine being

Devayana – the path of light that can be taken by the spirit after leaving the physical body

Devi – female deity, goddess

Dharana – concentration or complete attention; sixth stage of ashtanga yoga described by Patanjali's Yoga Sutras as holding or binding the mind to one point

Dhyana – spontaneous state after deep concentration or meditation; the seventh stage described in raja yoga

Dharma – the natural role one plays in life; ethical law; duty; regarded as one of the four aims of human existence

Dhauti – hatha yoga cleansing technique for the alimentary canal, stomach and sphincter muscle

Durga – remover of difficulties, the beautiful goddess who slays the difficult and even impossible enemies and rides the lion or tiger; the higher state of human consciousness and evolution

Dwapara yuga – the third aeon of the world, consisting of 864,000 years

Dwesha – repulsion, aversion, hatred; one of the five causes of suffering

Ekadashi – 11th day of the lunar fortnight, a time when mantra chanting and dietary restraint are held to be beneficial

Guna – quality, attribute or characteristic of all creation

Guru – one who dispels the darkness caused by ignorance (avidya); teacher; preceptor; teacher of the science of ultimate reality who, because of extended practice and previous attainment of the highest states of meditation, is fit to guide others in their practice towards enlightenment

Gurukul – educational system of ancient India, where children lived in the ashram or family of the guru and were taught a comprehensive syllabus for life by the guru

Hamsa – swan; third stage of sannyasa, emphasizing solitary sadhana

Hari – a name of Vishnu, one of the gods of the Hindu trinity composed of Brahma, the creator, Vishnu, the preserver, and Shiva, the destroyer

Harmonium – musical instrument like a small accordion, used in kirtan

Hatha yoga – a system of yoga dealing with practices for bodily purification; yoga of attaining physical and mental purity and balancing the prana (energy) in ida and pingala nadis so that sushumna nadi opens, enabling samadhi experiences

Ida nadi – channel of lunar energy between the left nostril and the base of the spine, governing the left side of the body and the right side of the brain

Indriya – sense organ

Ishta – object of desire; the chosen ideal; the particular form of God one is devoted to; worshipped, reverenced, beloved

Ishta devata – personal deity, one's favourite god

Ishta mantra – mantra of the chosen deity

Japa – to rotate or repeat continuously without a break; repetition of a mantra or name of God

Jivanmukta – a soul who is liberated while living

Jnana – awareness, knowledge and experience

Jnana yoga – yoga of knowledge and wisdom attained through spontaneous self-analysis and investigation of abstract ideas; contemplation as the principal means of attaining the higher knowledge of reality

Jnani – one who expresses wisdom in daily life

Kaivalya – final liberation

Kali yuga – the age of Kali, which lasts 432,000 years and is the fourth and current era (yuga) of the world now more than 5,000 years old, the 'iron' age, dark, evil, difficult and full of strife

Kalpa taru – 'wish fulfilling tree'; a psychic centre activated when anahata chakra is awakened, resulting in the ability to materialize what is desired

Karma – action and result; action in the manifest and unmanifest dimensions; work, duty

Karma sannyasa – householder sannyasa; renunciation combined with duty

Kathopanishad – one of the principal Upanishads belonging to the Taittiriya Brahmana of the Yajurveda, written in verse and dialogue form, in which the seeker Nachiketa speaks with Yama, the god of death

Kirtan – singing of God's name; practice in which a group of people sing a collection of mantras

Krishna – eighth incarnation of Vishnu. His teachings to his friend and disciple Arjuna are immortalized in the *Bhagavad Gita*

Kriya yoga – practices of kundalini yoga designed to speed the evolution of humanity

Kundalini – spiritual energy; the form of divine cosmic energy lying dormant in mooladhara chakra

Laya – dissolution

Likhit japa – practice of writing mantra

Mahamrityunjaya mantra – mantra used to avoid calamities

Maha siddhas – the great masters who are considered to be beyond the confines of time and space

Maha yajna – supreme sacrifice

Mala – rosary, string of beads used as a tool in the practice of mantra repetition

Mandala – diagram within a circumference symbolizing the deeper aspects of the human psyche and capable of invoking cosmic power

Mantra – subtle sound vibration; tantric tool which liberates energy fom the confines of mundane awareness and expands the consciousness when repeated

Maya – illusion; duality; cause of the phenomenal world

Mitahara – balanced, moderate diet

Moksha – final liberation

Mooladhara chakra – the basic psychic and pranic centre in the human body situated in the perineum in men and the cervix in women; seat of kundalini (the primal evolutionary energy in human beings)

Mouna – silence; measured silence, remaining silent for a specified span of time

Mridanga – two-sided drum

Mudra –physical, mental and psychic attitude which expresses and channels cosmic energy

Mumukshutva – desire for liberation, intense longing for liberation; fourth kind of necessary spiritual effort

Naam sankirtan – singing the name of God in a group

Naam smarana –remembrance of the Lord through repetition of His Name

Nadi shodhana pranayama – a pranayama which purifies and balances ida and pingala nadis by alternate nostril breathing

Navavidha bhakti – the nine modes of devotion

Nigama – vedic knowledge; ritual procedures

Nirvikalpa samadhi – state in which the mind ceases to function and only pure consciousness remains

Nivritti – renunciation of the external world

Niyama –observances or rules of personal discipline to render the mind tranquil in preparation for meditation; the second step of ashtanga yoga

Ojas – vitality, subliminal sexual energy

Paramahamsa sannyasa – stage of sannyasa where, having completed their work, paramahamsa sannyasins approach the final goal of moksha or self-realization

Patanjali –author of the Yoga Sutras

Pawanmuktasana – a group of asanas which remove any blockages preventing the free flow of energy in the body and mind

Pingala nadi – a major pranic channel in the body which conducts the dynamic pranic force manifesting as prana shakti, and governs the right side of the body and left side of the brain

Pitriyana – path of darkness

Prakriti – individual nature; manifest and unmanifest nature; cosmic energy; the active principle of manifest energy; nature or primordial matter (source of the universe)

Prana – breath, respiration; vital energy that functions in various ways for the preservation of the body and is closely associated with the mind

Pranava – another word for the sacred syllable Aum (Om)

Pranayama – a series of techniques using the breath to control the flow of prana within the body; expansion of the range of vital energy

Prarthana – worship through prayer

Pratipaksha bhavana – principle of yoga which states that one may control a negative emotion by summoning its opposite, or a lower thought by countering it with a higher one

Pratyahara – restraining the sensory and motor organs; withdrawal and emancipation of the mind from the domination of the senses and sensual objects; training the senses to follow the mind within

Pravritti – total involvement in the external world

Purusha – pure consciousness, unlimited by contact with prakriti or matter

Raga – love, affection; attachment, attraction

Raja yoga – yoga of awakening the psychic awareness and faculties through meditation

Rajas – one of the three gunas representing the dynamic, active state of mind and nature

Sadhaka – one who practises sadhana; spiritual aspirant, seeker

Sadhana – spiritual practice or discipline performed regularly for the attainment of inner experience

Saguna Brahman – forms of God; Brahman with attributes

Sakshi – eternal witness; witnessing principle

Samadhi – culmination of meditation; state of unity with the object of meditation and the universal consciousness; final step of raja yoga

Samatvam – equilibrium or equanimity, the greatest virtue for success in sadhana

Samsara – the manifest gross world; cycle of birth, death and rebirth

Sankalpa – will, positive resolve; purpose; determination, conviction

Sannyasa – dedication; complete renunciation of the world

Satchidananda – the supreme reality as self-existent existence-consciousness-bliss

Satsang – gathering in which the ideals and principles of truth are discussed; spiritual association; association with the wise and the good, along with the resolve and effort to express this in life

Sattwa – one of the three constituent qualities (gunas) of nature (prakriti) and all matter; state of luminosity, harmony, equilibrium, steadiness and purity

Satya – truthfulness

Satya yuga – the age in which piety and righteousness predominated and the first of the four aeons (yugas) of the world, the 'golden' age lasting for 1,728,000 years

Shadsampatti – sixfold virtues necessary for a serious spiritual aspirant: equanimity (shama), self-control (dama), sensory withdrawal (uparati), endurance (titiksha), faith (shraddha), constant concentration on reality (samadhana)

Shakti – primal energy; manifest consciousness; power, ability, capacity, strength, energy; the moving power of nature and consciousness

200

Shaktipat – higher energy or experience transmitted by the guru to a worthy disciple; descent of power through worship

Shama – tranquillity; mental quietness

Shiva – 'auspicious one; name of the god entrusted with the work of destroying the ego and duality; cosmic consciousness

Shiva Samhita – Sanskrit text enumerating the concepts and principles essential to the practice of yoga; classical textbook on hatha yoga

Shivalingam – black oval-shaped stone; symbol of Lord Shiva; symbol of consciousness

Shoonyata – void state of transcendental consciousness

Siddha – perfected being; sage, seer; accomplished soul

Siddhi – paranormal or supernatural accomplishment; control of mind and prana; psychic ability

Stuti – singing the praises of the Lord

Sushumna nadi – central energy flow (nadi) in the spine which conducts the kundalini or spiritual force from mooladhara chakra to sahasrara chakra; main energy flow related to transcendental awareness

Swaroopa – one's own form or shape, essential nature

Swadhyaya – self-study; continuous conscious awareness of what one is doing

Tamas – inertia, stability; ignorance, darkness; one of the three constituent qualities (gunas) of nature (prakriti), in yoga it is characterized by inertia, laziness, mental dullness, unwillingness to change

Tantra – most ancient universal science incorporating innumerable practices for the expansion of mind and liberation of energy

Tapas – austerity; process of burning the impurities; in yoga means a burning effort which involves purification, self-discipline and austerity

Titiksha – endurance, bearing heat and cold and other pairs of opposites without complaint; one of the sixfold virtues

Treta yuga – the second of the four aeons of the world, lasting for 1,296,000 years; an aeon where goodness is on the increase leading up to Satya yuga

Tyaga – renunciation or gradual dissociation of the mind from worldly objects and the seed of desire

Ujjayi pranayama – 'psychic breathing'; pranayama which internalizes the awareness and induces meditative states

Upanishad – ancient vedic texts containing intimate dialogues and discussions between guru and disciple on the nature of the absolute and the path leading towards it

Upaya – approach, means; effort; tantra has four main upaya sadhanas: anavopaya, shaktopaya, shambhavopaya, anupaya (although anupaya requires no means or effort)

Vairagya – non-attachment, dispassion, detachment from the world and its cause

Vasana – subtle impressions acting like seeds in the mind capable of germinating or developing into action

Vedanta – philosophy of realization of Brahman

Vedas – the most ancient and sacred literature of the Hindus, dealing with the nature of human beings and the universe

Vichara – reflection; enquiry into the nature of the self, Brahman or truth

Vidya – higher knowledge, right knowledge, spiritual knowledge

Virya – the essence of life; splendour, lustre; the result of mastering brahmacharya according to Patanjali's *Yoga Sutras*

Viveka – discrimination; right knowledge or understanding; sense of discrimination between the eternal and the transitory

Vritti – a modification arising in consciousness; the five mental modifications described in Patanjali's Yoga Sutras are: right knowledge (pramana), wrong knowledge (viparyaya), dream or fancy (vikalpa), sleep (nidra) and memory (smriti)

Yajna – sacrifice or sacrificial rite; yajna has three components: ritual or worship (pooja), satsang and unconditional giving (dana)

Yama – self-restraints or rules of conduct which render the emotions tranquil

Yantra – geometric symbol designed for concentration or meditation

Yoga nidra – 'psychic sleep'; a state of complete bodily relaxation in which the mind rests in a suspended state

Yoga Sutras – ancient authoritative text on yoga by Sage Patanjali

Yuga – aeon, age; according to yogic understanding advanced civilizations have risen and fallen many times as the universe pulsates through phases of evolution and manifestation and phases of involution or dissolution There are four aeons of the world; Satya yuga, Treta yuga, Dwapara yuga and Kali yuga